S0-AYT-107

The Secret to "I AM"

Also By Susan K. Wehrley

Books
The Secret to "I AM"
Discover Your Story . . . Discover Your Purpose

The Secret to "I AM"
Wisdom Tips and Workbook

Audio Programs
The Secret to "I AM"
Wisdom Tips CD

Videotapes
The Secret to "I AM"
Sensory Seminar

The Secret to "I AM"
A True Story

Discover Courage, Truth, Purpose, and Peace in Difficult Times

By Susan K. Wehrley

Thomas
& Kay

This is a true story. However, some of the names and identifying details relating to certain individuals have been changed in order to protect their privacy. All other descriptions have been recalled to the best of the author's ability.

Copyright © 2003 by Susan K. Wehrley. All rights reserved. No part of this book may be reproduced or transmitted in any form or by any means, electronic or mechanical, including photocopying, recording, or by information storage and retrieval systems, without the written permission of the publisher.

Publisher:
Thomas & Kay, LLC
250 North Sunnyslope Road, Suite 300
Brookfield, WI. 53005

Editing by Stephanie Gunning
Illustrations by Karen M. Wiltz
Book Interior by Tricia C. Young

FIRST EDITION

ISBN 0-9729505-0-8
ISBN (Limited Keepsake Edition) 0-9729505-2-4

10 9 8 7 6 5 4 3 2 1

For my daughters,
Alex and Lisa . . .

May the secret to "I AM"
live within you always!

Contents

Acknowledgements

There are so many people I want to thank for their love and support throughout the creation of this book and throughout my personal journey:

My mother . . . for giving me life and being a business role model.

My father, Donald . . . for expressing his belief in me.

My Aunt, Sister Mary Nora Barber . . . for being a spiritual role model.

My family and friends: Lisa, Alex, Gary, Jon, Peggy, Sam, Nan, Lisa, and Maureen–thank you for your love and support as I journeyed through the Four Secrets to "I AM."

My bible study friends: Lori, Kathy, and Marjorie– without your support I would never have discovered the Fourth Secret.

My teachers: Lori Gramling, Ingrid Lawrenz, David Hubbard, and Monica Ennis . . . for your wisdom, support, and unconditional love as I learned lessons along the way.

Tom, who taught me the many aspects of love.

And, above all, to God. It has only been through Him that all things were possible!

The Secret to "I AM"

"For you created my inmost being;
you knit me together in my mother's womb.
I praise you because I am fearfully
and wonderfully made;
your works are wonderful,
I know that full well.
My frame was not hidden from you
when I was made in the secret place.
When I was woven together in the depths of the earth,
your eyes saw my unformed body.
All the days ordained for me
were written in your book
before one of them came to be."

Psalm 139: 13-16

Introduction

Several years ago, I noticed that the self-help sections of bookstores were expanding. More books promised to answer the question: How can I live a better life? I bought and read many of these, as I searched for my own answers. In the process, it occurred to me that although members of our society spend billions of dollars on books, tapes, and seminars telling us how to improve our bodies, health, finances, jobs, and relationships, too many of us wonder why we aren't feeling fulfilled despite this information.

For years, I continued to seek knowledge, even as I became overwhelmed and worn out by the multitude of products promising me a better way to live. Ultimately, I wondered, *Is there such a thing as an information junkie?* If so, I had discovered my addiction: The need to find answers outside of myself.

The Secret to "I AM" A True Story: Discover Courage, Truth, Purpose, and Peace in Difficult Times takes a different approach. Instead of telling you how to live your life, I have chosen to share the intimate story of how I was finally able to live a life of courage, truth, purpose, and peace by looking inwardly and to God for answers.

My life story unfolded along with my struggle to answer the question: Who am I? Although I began searching for my identity by looking for my biological father, my quest subsequently evolved into a profound personal and spiritual journey that taught me how to face pain and uncertainty with courage. Over the years, the sense of connection that I've developed with and through myself, others, and the great "I AM" God presence has offered me an extraordinary amount of peace and fulfillment. In hindsight, it's clear to me that the purpose of my path was to discover the Four Secrets to living with a heart wide open to love. Today, I lead seminars and give lectures to teach these universal principles.

Even if the specific circumstances of your life are very different than mine, the journey for all of us is a familiar one. Everyone faces difficult times upon occasion. We all have our own struggles to overcome, purposes to discover, and questions to answer. As you read *The Secret to "I AM"*, you'll see that once the secret of my parentage was revealed, that's when my real, deeper journey began. Over many years, I progressed from self-denial, to self-awareness, to self-love, and, ultimately, to trusting in a Higher Power. That journey continues today.

Powerful possibilities exist for all of us whenever we find the courage to embrace our unique experience, the unknown, our intuitive wisdom, and a love in something bigger than ourselves. My hope is that my true story inspires you to manifest the glory of God within, by being all you can be in each moment of your life.

May God bless you richly on your personal journey of transformation.

Susan

Susan K. Wehrley

The First Secret:

Embrace Your Uniqueness

It is what it is,
You are who you are;
So instead of fighting
It, start exploring . . .

ASK:
"Hmm . . . Isn't that interesting . . . I wonder?"

The Courage to Explore Self-doubt

Looking back, I can see the loving and masterful orchestration that transformed my life from one filled with deception, adversity, and fear to one of courageous possibilities and love. This is a journey that everyone has the opportunity to take. We're ready for a major shift when we begin facing the deep questions we've always wondered about.

Most of us have a "tip of the iceberg" cue that causes us to question aspects of our lives. For me, the initial obvious trait was my physical appearance. This made me curious about a family secret that I believed held the answer to my identity. While all the other members of my family were short and dark-haired, by fourth grade I was already five-foot four-inches tall with long, wavy blonde hair and a fair complexion. This contrast made me feel awkward. I wondered, *Why am I so different?* It wasn't until much later that I realized that the quest to know myself biologically would offer a deeper emotional and spiritual message about the enormous power of love, forgiveness, and compassion to heal our wounds.

My curiosity often got me in trouble as a kid, especially with my mother. My questions were like a thorn in her side. When I asked her where my physical traits came from, instead of giving me reassurance and direct answers she became defensive, which made me wonder even more.

Like most children, my nature was to be curious and aware. Unfortunately, self-doubt replaced the inner knowing that otherwise was so natural. An inner wound was created when the magnificent power of my curiosity and insight was squelched by adults whose shame dismissed these gifts within me.

When we are young and there's a condition in our families or an event takes place that's not discussed, we don't learn how to put words to what's happening around and within us. As a result of such family secrets, we face a fork in the road—we either choose to connect with the denial of our parents so we can have their approval, or we choose to connect with our selves, thus learning to embrace our intuitive wisdom and the wealth of love offered from within us.

At this age, choosing our own truth and self-connection over the truth of and connection with a person upon whom we are dependent is very scary. Although we intuitively know that something is wrong, our lack of language to articulate our perceptions, needs, and feelings makes us susceptible later in life. Gone unchecked, we'll carry the unconscious emotions that no one's talking about long into our adulthood. In fact, until we re-experience these feelings, find a language to describe them, and see them through the eyes of compassion and love, we'll continually be challenged by them.

As a child, the question I asked that irritated my mother the most was, "Is Dad my real dad?"

"Don't be silly! Why would you think such a ridiculous thing?" she would answer, very annoyed that I would even dare to wonder and ask. "It must be your imagination," she would add.

My mother's angry denials made me feel less willing to trust my instincts. This initiated a tendency to squelch my confidence and dismiss my sense of reality, even though I knew deep down that something wasn't "right." While I tried to bury my pain and ignore the nagging feelings I had inside, for years they would keep resurfacing in broken relationships that had one common denominator: me!

4

Later in life, my healing journey would include the lesson of learning how to honor myself as well as someone else. I needed to learn how to stay open, curious, connected, articulate, and loving, rather than dismissing things that didn't feel good to me, burying my feelings, and quitting. Embracing my unique self, including my personal perceptions, questions, and emotional experience, was going to be a part of that incredible journey.

I took all the detours available to me to delay learning this lesson for years. Although I never abused addictive substances like alcohol and drugs, without realizing it, I developed alternative patterns of avoiding pain. For instance, I would look outside of myself and fantasize about "love and marriage" and a "wonderful career." My illusions gave me the promise of "happily ever after."

The first time I thought I'd found the key to "happily ever after" was when a girlfriend spotted a picture of a guy she liked posted on the wall at the college we attended. As she pointed him out, she gasped over his good looks and informed me that his name was Steve and he was on the golf team. Although my friend staked her claim on wanting to go out with him, I decided to jump in the game as well. Her interest in him made me feel interested. Not knowing much about relationships other than to judge them by appearances, I thought, *Wow! This guy has a lot going for him. I want him too!* Not only did I tell my friend that I wanted to go out with Steve, I upped the ante on her, saying, "I'm going to marry him some day!"

Interestingly enough, I had the opportunity to meet Steve a week later when my roommates and I were out celebrating my 21st birthday. There he was, standing tall among the crowd at almost six-foot-three. He happened to be with a mutual friend, making it easy to go over and chat. Not much revealing was shared, as the hour was late. But we exchanged a lot of laughs. After a while, the bar lights went on. The night was over. As I was leaving, I announced that I wanted a birthday kiss from all of my friends, including one from Steve. There wasn't anything particularly magical about it. In fact, I couldn't remember it.

Two nights later, I went out to the local bar with one of my friends. After having had too many celebration shots earlier in the week, this time I was drinking soda. I caught a glimpse of Steve as he walked in. He wished me a happy birthday again and somehow referred to our kiss.

"We kissed?" I asked. For a moment, I wondered why I didn't remember the kiss. Although I'd been drinking, it wasn't to the point that I'd forgotten the events of the night. *How strange,* I thought.

"Yes, we did," Steve said, looking in my eyes seriously.

Suddenly, I was distracted. My girlfriend who'd claimed her desire for him in the hall a few weeks earlier, sat beside us drooling. There was flirting going on in front of me and jealousy took over. Now, I was more tuned in to competition, and overriding their connection, than what was authentically going on inside of me. By the end of the night I had met my first goal . . . *I* had a date with the guy whose picture was hanging on the wall.

That's how I found myself, one year later, at age 22, married to someone I hardly knew. "How did that happen?" you may ask. I got swept up in everyone's awe over what a beautiful couple they thought we made. While deep down I doubted the relationship, I deceived myself about how I really felt. I wondered, *What's wrong with me that I can't love him as much as everyone else seems to?*

People often referred to Steve and I as "Barbie and Ken" because we appeared so perfectly matched on the outside. Yet, on the inside we weren't connected at all. At that point, I didn't even know that two people had more to offer one another. Truthfully, I didn't have anything more to offer to myself, let alone my husband, because I was so disconnected within. I was impressed by outer appearances and other people's opinions, and this eventually led me to betray myself.

I gave my life over to Steve's dreams and goals, which he had clearly mapped out. This allowed me to continue doing what I'd been taught subliminally at home: "Don't search within to find the passions and truths of your own heart and soul. Please and impress others instead." Rather than exploring my life's path I found refuge in someone else's. I was hiding.

How was I to learn how to undo my deeply ingrained self-deceit and self-betrayal? It wasn't until three years into my marriage that I knew I was living a life that wasn't my own. I started to abandon my own needs and dreams when I decided to transfer out of the college that Steve and I both attended so that I could be with him in Milwaukee where he got a job. By the middle of my senior year of college, we were married. Six weeks later, I found out I was pregnant with a "honeymoon baby," much to my surprise. This took my life on an unexpected turn.

Steve got a job working for a Big Eight accounting firm, which had him traveling Monday through Friday. While I finished up school and later stayed home raising our infant daughter Lisa, he was trying to establish his career so that he could become a partner some day. He continually tried to reassure me that this was what we needed and that it would be worth it in the end some day. But I felt lonely and resentful. I was very young and it was tough on me.

For months, I begged Steve to get another job. He told me that staying with the firm would be good for us; we both just needed to ride it out. The night I called him in his hotel room was the night I concluded I no longer could. I'd just put Lisa to bed and I was feeling lonely. When he answered the phone, I could hear the TV on in the background. He was watching a ball game and seemed wrapped up in what he was doing. Then, I also heard a woman's voice. I was shocked and asked him,

"Who was that?"

Steve acted as though it was no big deal and said, "It's the girl I'm working with on this project. We're having pizza and watching the game in my room so we can finish before morning."

I was speechless. Being only 23 and inexperienced made me doubt whether I had the right to be angry with my husband or to have expected him to make a different choice. I wondered, *What does the business world expect of its employees? Was I supposed to play the role of the understanding wife who just "rode" that out too?* At that moment I said nothing other than, "Well, I'll let you go." I hoped he would sense my hurt and irritation, but he didn't.

How did I get here? I wondered. Had I missed all the signs and opportunities along the way that told me this road–this marriage–would be a dead-end for me? I felt like Sleeping Beauty waiting to be awakened by some person or some power outside of myself. I wasn't sure what to do, what to say, or where to turn. I was miserable.

While I was beginning to doubt my decision to marry Steve, he was becoming increasingly busy, uncommunicative, and distant. It was possible that he'd acted like that from the beginning and I'd just never noticed. The only choice I felt was available to me was to get on with creating a life that would be fulfilling. But how would I do that? I was never taught how to go deep within and explore my feelings, to overcome my fears, and to manifest my dreams. On the other hand, I was taught how to notice everyone else's feelings and needs and to compromise my own. So, here was an opportunity for me to be curious and embrace my unique self. But, instead of dealing with my discontent with Steve, or deeply exploring what would make me fulfilled, I quickly decided that getting a job would be the answer.

Although I initially intended to get a job I desired, I soon doubted whether that was really fair with a newborn at home and a traveling husband. Because I was unsure about what I felt was right, I was quickly consumed with the opinions and feelings of my in-laws, and husband, who strongly believed it was a mother's job to stay home with her child. So when I began to look in the newspaper for a job, I negated any job that would mean Lisa would have to go to a babysitter.

The job I really wanted was to be a motivational speaker. That had been my ambition since I was 16 years old. Many Sunday afternoons were spent watching incredible speakers on TV like Leo Buscaglia and Zig Ziglar, wishing that someday I could make the same kind of difference in the world. Yet, the dream seemed too far to reach.

I compromised by choosing to work for a national real estate company that owned several apartment communities around town. They'd advertised for someone willing to work as a part-time sales and renovation manager for a 240-unit apartment community. They were offering a modest salary, but it included the free rental of one of the apartments, which also would be my home office. Although the salary was less than ideal and the job was not what my heart desired, I concluded that I was doing the right thing to work out of my home. Yet, deep down I still felt a void and disconnection from my strong ambition to make a difference in the world.

It's funny though how our essence is not defined by our circumstances or by our job in life. Although my job wasn't the motivational speaker position I had hoped for when I graduated, it wasn't long into my new job before I could see how I was able to influence others and quickly manifest change around me. I thought, *This feels pretty good!* I gained the favorable attention of my boss, who made it very clear to the whole company that I was the new star employee. He was impressed with how I turned an apartment community from 78 percent to 97 percent occupancy in a short period of time, and I was flattered by his attention. Positive attention was something that I didn't know how to give myself or get from my husband, so it sure felt good.

After working for the company for almost two years, I was offered a promotion. If I took it, I would become National Sales Director and oversee 2,000 properties. This meant that I would have to travel with my boss, Gary, whom I was beginning secretly to admire. But, even at my young age, I had the sense that this wouldn't be a good idea. After taking the risk to tell my husband that I was becoming attracted to someone else and distracted from our marriage, I suggested to him that I would quit my job. He responded the way he usually did . . . he didn't show any emotion. Still, I quit. Despite that conversation, he continued to travel and be emotionally and physically unavailable.

On my birthday that year, months later, my husband was working in Madison, only an hour from where we lived in Milwaukee. Even though it was a Wednesday evening, I asked him to please come home so we could celebrate together. He responded by telling me how overwhelmed he was with work and that we would celebrate when he came home for the weekend.

Tired of being at home, I first called my mother to watch my daughter and then called my friend Peggy to see if she wanted to go out. Peggy and I were best friends and had known each other since seventh grade. She was the only person who knew of the loneliness in my marriage, while everyone else was still being fooled by the beautiful appearance we put on.

Peggy and I decided to go out to a local restaurant called Saz's to celebrate. When we arrived, my old boss Gary and some of my other former co-workers from the real estate company just happened to be there. They asked us to join them and, because I was starving for some fun, we continued the evening by following them to another bar across town where there was a live band playing. Dancing was my favorite hobby, so I knew I'd have a great time. In the past, I'd been a pom-pom girl in college as well as a contest-winning disco "queen."

As the night went on, the drinks were plentiful. I began to forget about how lonely I felt. Being out on the dance floor brought me back to my exciting college days. The music changed tempo. Gary asked if I wanted to slow dance, and with a smile grabbed my hand to pull me close to his body. It had been a long time since I remembered feeling as alive. For a few moments, I could escape.

Two slow dances later, it was closing time and Gary and his friend walked Peggy and me to our car. "I have Bucks tickets on Sunday. Do you want to join me and some of the people at work for the game?" he asked me.

"Sure," I said, feeling flattered by the attention.

"Okay . . . great. I'll pick you up at noon."

He kissed me and gave me a hug as we said good-bye. Peggy and I got into the car. As we drove away, it took me a few blocks before reality set in.

"What just happened?" I asked. "I accepted an invitation to a basketball game with Gary. What am I thinking? I'm married!" I was so disconnected from my marriage that, in the moment, I'd felt like a single woman. I couldn't believe what I'd just done and couldn't figure out how I was going to handle it.

Finally, I confided in my mother. I told her how very unhappy I was in my marriage and that I was beginning to be attracted to my former boss. I told her about the incident in the parking lot and how confused it made me. Her advice was, "If you need to see him, do it and get it out of your system. Just don't get a divorce."

That advice seemed odd. Although I didn't know myself well, one thing I did know was that it was difficult for me to lie outwardly. My marriage may have been inauthentic, but treating Steve with this level of deception was something I couldn't handle.

I canceled my plans to go to the Sunday basketball game and again pleaded with my husband to quit his job. This time I shared with him in more detail how terribly lonely I felt and how I was beginning to feel attracted to Gary. He only commented on my request for him to quit. Steve remained steadfast and focused on what he thought was best for us. "You'll be happy in the long run," he kept repeating.

At some level, I could sense the message was: "Forget you have feelings and desires. Stick with me and you'll live happily ever after." But again I didn't know how to put my perceptions into words, so I couldn't discuss the real conversation with him that was unspoken.

Instead of having an honest and open conversation, I did what I knew how to do, I doubted myself and bought into the illusion. Putting myself aside for the promise of "happily-ever-after" hooked me for another two months, until I finally couldn't take the internal pressure anymore of pushing down my own truth. Eventually, the truth popped out like a Jack-in-the-box. Again, I did the only thing I knew how to do. To regain control, I announced, "That's it, I've had it . . . I am filing for divorce."

My family was appalled at how I could divorce such a "fine, hard-working, and good-looking man." They told me that it was wrong, that I was Catholic, and that I had taken vows for better or for worse. Frankly, I found their strong opinions and criticism hypocritical, since most of the people in my family had been divorced, including my parents, who'd been divorced since I was young.

Inside, I felt lonely, isolated, scared, and rejected–but I didn't know where to turn. I still hadn't learned how to deeply embrace and connect with my inner experiences. I felt confused, not knowing what I wanted out of life, and, worse yet, not believing I could get it. Because I was filled with so much self-doubt, I didn't know how to work through and embrace these difficult feelings. How was I to become clear and connect within so that I could embrace who I was?

Unfortunately, my hopelessness kept me from going inward to embrace and understand my pain. Instead, I took the first outward opportunity to soothe the pain, when Gary called after he found out that I'd filed for divorce. Within weeks, I found myself entangled in a relationship with him, even though I hadn't moved out of the house yet.

Although I was making the choice to see Gary before my divorce was final, I knew this choice was not congruent with my code of ethics. I was experiencing guilt and judgment toward myself for not being strong enough to wait until the relationship was completely over between Steve and I. For me, being in a relationship with someone else before the divorce was final was a strong "not" goal that had an unusual magnitude to it, beyond religious implications. Because I had focused for so long to not divorce or to "not" be needy, or "not" cheat, I ended up created a self-fulfilling prophecy. Because I didn't know what it actually was that I wanted, I couldn't manifest it.

I continued to be confused and looked for a connection outside of myself. After three months, Gary and I became physically involved on the night before he left for the Super Bowl in Florida. I felt so open and connected that I was sure it was right or it wouldn't have felt so good. Physical attraction, chemistry, and sexual compatibility were the only barometers I was aware of at the time for a relationship. *Is there something else that would create a lasting connection?* I occasionally wondered. The only other bonds I knew about were common interests and goals, which we seemed to have as well.

A few days later, Gary flew to Florida with his boss and their two corporate attorneys. I was off to my uncle's house for a Super Bowl party. I couldn't wait to share with my family how I was doing so much better now that

I had met this great guy. About halfway into the party, just as I was telling my uncle about Gary, something caught my attention and drew me to the TV screen. I couldn't believe my eyes. There sat Gary with his boss and two blonde women, one on each side of them.

I felt devastated, foolish, and powerless. Could I believe my eyes? Was that really Gary on TV? My first immediate thoughts went to self-judgment: *How could I have been so wrong as to believe that we had something special between us?* These two women hanging on the arms of Gary and his boss didn't look like corporate attorneys to me.

I quickly found an excuse to leave the family party, not knowing how to share this turn of events with anyone. Two days later, when Gary returned to Milwaukee, I confronted him. Initially he lied and said it wasn't true. It wasn't until I told him that we could go over to my uncle's together and see what the Super Bowl videotape revealed that he chose to tell the truth. He justified his behavior by telling me that the plans with his boss and the women were made prior to getting involved with me. He told me that he didn't know how to disappoint either his boss or me, so he chose just to "handle it on his own," which he thought would end up fine.

I didn't know how to be with my thoughts of judgment and feelings of fear and deep betrayal at the time. Deception was difficult for me to handle. So I did what I knew how to do . . . I broke up with him. That gave me a temporary feeling of relief and power until the loneliness and confusion set in again.

My pain was growing deeper, yet I still didn't know how to work through the intense feelings that were consuming me. People suggested that maybe I had made the wrong decision to leave my unavailable, yet stable husband. I was beginning to wonder myself, so I ended up getting back together with Steve to see if we could mend our differences.

Deep down inside I was scared. All I could see were two options: being with someone who was safe and unavailable, or being with someone who seemed exciting but could potentially break my heart. With only those two options in my awareness, I chose the first for the time being.

Needless to say, after six months and no progress in my marriage, I was right back where I started. Steve and I were still disconnected, but now it was worse. He felt he couldn't trust me and his fear was surfacing by following me around and checking up on me regularly to see if I had reconnected with Gary. I didn't know how to soothe his hurt and insecurity, as I had so much of my own pain, which was neglected the first time around in our relationship. But now the focus was on me. I was the one that had left him and who got involved with someone else before the divorce was final.

I honestly wanted Steve and I to discover a way to cross over the wall of self-protection we'd built between us, but I simply didn't know how to do it. Instead, I did what I knew how to do: I took on the anxiety and shame for the both of us, and pushed down my own sense of truth. There I was, saying how much I hated my life, yet I could not see my responsibility in creating the life I didn't want because I still didn't know how to embrace who I was and what it was I really wanted. Because I felt so lost and confused, I was quickly looking for an answer to soothe my pain. This time I chose to file for divorce.

At this point, I was bound and determined to handle my divorce differently. I was going to go off on my own and find myself and discover who I was. But how was I going to do that? I had no idea . . .

2

The Courage to Connect
with Who I Am

Around the time my marriage ended, I landed a new job. I'd been working in the advertising department of a community newspaper. The printer of the paper had just been given an opportunity to print for a large direct mail company that was opening up a new branch in town. He called me into his office one day and asked if I was interested in interviewing with his new client.

"You could more than double your income," he said. "They told me they're looking for someone who can sell, is good with people, and who has a desire to work hard and make money. I thought of you. I also figured that more income might come in handy since you're going through a divorce."

He was right; I was interested in advancing my career. Being a single woman at age 25 with a young daughter was scary. So I interviewed and got the job. I pulled up my bootstraps to make things work. Although I wasn't seeing anyone at the time, I still felt distracted from being with myself at a deep level. Ending up in business and intuitively knowing what I needed to do to succeed in a male-dominated profession kept me from turning inward towards my feelings.

Early on in this high-pressure job, I learned an important business rule: Don't bring your personal life or emotions to work. It was challenging. Although I was out of touch with my emotions much of the time, it was an enormously difficult task to separate my talent and logic from my emotions, intuition, and spirit. One thing was for sure: if I wanted to be successful and support my daughter, and myself, I believed I had to "just do it."

It didn't take long before I was convinced that disconnecting from myself emotionally and trying harder was actually getting me somewhere. Within a few months, the company promoted me to head of Regional Sales. Of four new hires, I was the only one chosen to call on local companies that had regional or national headquarters in the Milwaukee/Chicago area. Sometimes I wondered what they saw in me. Was I as good as they thought I was or just good at pretending? I often felt a bit inadequate for the challenge.

Then, one day, when I had finally cracked my first big national account, I got a call at the office. It was Gary. He'd heard I was again getting a divorce. "Can we meet for lunch and just talk? I've missed you," he said in a soft, sweet voice.

Part of me wanted to say no, and part of me was touched by his desire for me. Although I was feeling fulfilled and appreciated at work, as a woman I was still feeling confused and lonely. So, I gave in to my desire and two days later we met for lunch. We both cried as we shared how much we'd missed each other and how the time apart didn't work out for either of us with other people.

That was the beginning of the relationship that became my second marriage.

Gary and I dated for almost a year before he moved into my home. Secretly, I was afraid of getting remarried only to end up in another divorce. At that time, I thought living together would surely be the wise thing to do before we made a commitment. But I'm not so sure that living together taught us anything. Still, within a year we were married. Beforehand, I knew that I had unresolved issues with trust in myself and in the relationship, yet I didn't know what to do about them. So, although I already knew I couldn't open my heart fully to him, I told myself that the relationship was as good as it gets.

Life was moving fast, as we both worked to advance

our relationship and our careers. He had now been promoted to Vice President of his real estate company. I was now the top salesperson in my region at my company, earning over six figures a year. Despite the earlier divorce, life seemed like it was working out–until I got pregnant with my second daughter. Being pregnant brought up feelings of anxiety and insecurity that I noticed but couldn't seem to explain at the time.

One day, when I was about eight months pregnant, I came home for lunch and sat in a brand-new chair in the living room. It was one of the only times I could remember being in the living room and doing nothing except relaxing. I looked around at the brand-new furniture, new blinds, and new white carpeting, and at my Mercedes convertible in the driveway, and I wondered, *Why am I not fulfilled?* I knew something was missing, but I didn't know what.

Growing up on the East Side near prestigious Lake Drive had led me to believe that the possessions around me were the things that would make me happy. After all, that's what I saw the adults I knew striving for when I was a kid. Now, at age 28, I supposedly had it all: a handsome husband, a beautiful home, a great car, a six-figure job, a sweet daughter, and another child on the way. But I didn't feel happy. I felt empty inside. Instead of pondering why my belongings and relationships weren't enough to fulfill me, I began to doubt myself. *Maybe something is wrong with me that I can't be satisfied.* Dismissing my feelings and judging myself was a pattern I hadn't yet learned to break.

Then, one month later, life presented an unexpected twist in the road. My second daughter had just been born and was in and out of the hospital with high fevers and colds. That meant sleepless nights for the entire family. It was the first time in my life that I was in touch with feeling out of control. I wondered, *Now what?* All I could think about was a commercial where a woman steps into a soothing bubble bath and says, "Calgon, take me away!" I wanted to flee from having to choose between pursuing my career and staying home with my sick daughter. All I could do was hope that her condition would go away . . . but it didn't!

My career responsibilities seemed too much to deal with, so I decided to take advantage of the three-month maternity leave that was available to me. It wasn't much more than four weeks later when I started receiving frequent phone calls from the office throughout the day. My boss was growing weary of the extra account load he was carrying while I was gone, and I was growing weary of all of the pressure I was feeling from the people around me.

Finally, after a few more weeks, my boss blew up. I couldn't help but wonder if he wasn't perhaps resentful as well as overworked. After all, from his point of view it looked as though I had all the freedom and made more money, while he was the one handling all the work. I began to feel pressure from all directions and couldn't see any options other than grin it and bear it or flee. I kept wondering, *What should I do?*

3

The Courage to Face
Confusion and Clear the Fog

After many sleepless days and nights, my inner conflict started getting to me. As my new daughter Alex was becoming sicker, so was I. Or was it the other way around? My sickness was in the form of people pleasing, losing my voice, and leaving no room to breathe. Hers came in the form of sinus infections, throat viruses, and sleepless nights. It's interesting how we were subtly mirroring each other.

Although, by law, I had the right to take off a full three months for maternity leave, I was beginning to feel guilty, so I asked the company if we could come up with a part-time arrangement until my daughter was better. The management agreed to allow me to work part-time if I would come back right away and if I gave half of my commissions to my boss who was handling my accounts while I was gone. So I did. Although I wasn't too happy about giving up part of my income, I rationalized the agreement by telling myself it was a compromise and a win-win solution for all concerned.

So, there I was, back at work again, making it happen before the three-month leave was officially over. I was there not because I wanted to be, but because I was afraid of losing all that I'd worked so hard to create.

In order to keep myself from experiencing my anxiety, I made myself into "Gumby Girl" by stretching myself to meet everyone's needs. (Gumby was an old children's toy that could bend and twist in many directions because it was made of rubber with a wire inside). There were my boss and clients who needed answers; my husband, who expected more of me now that he was traveling; and Alex, who was crying a lot in the background as if to say, "What about me?" Of course, there was also my oldest daughter Lisa, who was trying to figure out how she fit into our blended family with a new baby and into my priorities since I had a career that was getting a lot of my attention.

All those needs made going back to work difficult. I can remember hiding in the bathroom at the office almost every day for a few minutes so I could cry and release some of the pressure I was feeling. This was a time in business where job sharing and part-time at the executive level rarely existed. It was also a time when it was rare for a woman as young as I was to have such a high-paying, responsible job. I felt inadequate to handle it, but didn't know where to turn.

A female co-worker knew about my struggle and suggested that I quit working all together to be at home with Alex. I tried to explain to her that it wasn't that easy a choice. In addition to giving up the recognition and money I got from working, I wasn't sure at this point if I could survive going back to being a stay-at-home mom. Imagining being home full-time brought up memories of how vulnerable I'd felt when I was home alone with Lisa, my elder daughter.

As I pondered what to do, Alex grew sicker. Finally, after another big blow out with my boss one day, it was finally clear . . . I couldn't take the pressure anymore. I did what I always did when the going got tough . . . I quit my job.

On one level, it was difficult to leave my six-figure income, even though I was pretty exhausted. It's not that I didn't like what I was doing, because I did. I was comfortable with the lifestyle my income was providing and I enjoyed the recognition I got for my performance. Yet, my heart was crying to be home with my sick daughter and perhaps to venture out to do what I'd always wanted to do: become a motivational speaker. But

I was scared.

Performance was the only identity I had at that point. What if I went out on a limb only to fail? My husband liked my income and the security it provided. Taking a risk would mean we would have to give up investing in the future, which was very important to him. Again, I felt trapped between manifesting my dreams and pleasing someone else so they could have theirs.

Besides pleasing my husband, it was also difficult to imagine losing the approval of my family, who had changed from being ashamed of me for getting a divorce to being proud of me for making something out of my life. Yet, I wanted to enjoy life more, including taking the risk to manifest my dream and spending time caring for my new baby at home who was ill too often.

It took some adjusting at first, but within a few months of quitting my job my performance identity was beginning to melt away as a new sense of self emerged. Now, Alex was reflecting my inner peace back to me, as she was getting healthier and sleeping through the night. Oddly, her sickness had given me the courage to quit working so hard and to begin to examine my life.

I finally took the plunge and followed my heart's desire. I went into business for myself as a part-time corporate motivational and sales trainer. Life supported me by offering me more space to explore and connect with myself. My husband Gary had begun traveling to Florida every week to establish two new apartment communities that his company acquired. So, even though I was caring for two young kids at home, my schedule allowed me time to let my mind be quiet. The time I would have spent cleaning the house, preparing bigger meals, sitting and talking with my husband was now spent on just being with myself. I had room for my mind to take me where it needed to go, and to ponder, *What does life have in store for me?* Slowing down my pace and having some alone-time helped me switch from an outward focus to a more inward one.

Often, I found myself in deeper contemplation about the unresolved issues in my life, including the old, persistent question that haunted me: *Was my father really my biological father?*

One day, when I was out walking our dog, I found my mind reflecting back to a childhood memory . . .

I was riding with my dad in his red Blazer. As a child, I felt unstoppable on the road, big and on top of the world, as we rode together high above the other cars. I knew my father loved his truck . . . maybe that's why I also loved it so much. His self-assured and happy energy was appealing to me because his heart was wide open to life in that moment.

Since my parents were divorced, I'd spend a lot of time driving back and forth with him from the east side of town, where my mother lived, to the west side of town, where he lived. When he and I were alone in the truck, the two of us would sing his favorite country tunes. Country music never particularly appealed to me, however singing with my father did, especially when his favorite song came on. "Come live with me and be my life . . ." He would get excited, turn up the music, and–on nice days–roll down the window, all in one motion.

As I walked, my mind then drifted to a beautiful summer day when I was 16 years old. The sky was blue and the air a perfect 72 degrees, with a slight breeze, creating an enjoyable aroma from my mother's garden. I was outside waiting for my dad, as he drove up in his red truck to get me for the weekend. This time I was again alone with him as I hopped in and we quickly proceeded down the road. It was one of those days where my heart was wide open and everything felt wonderful, safe, and complete. Suddenly an urge came over me and I turned to my father and asked him the question that I had wondered for years, "Are you my real father?"

Dad looked amazed, stunned, and scared. I felt like I

could almost hear his thoughts radiate from his heart to mine. I was sure he was wondering, *How did you know?*

I took a deep breath then, knowing the answer to my question, but wishing it would be different. I had asked him, although I really didn't want to hear the truth. As my question lingered in the air, I looked back at Dad, my eyes pleading with him to tell me it wasn't true. I'm confident he could feel my mixed emotions. Part of me wanted to know, even though I wished it wasn't true.

Noticing my ambiguity, Dad took a deep breath. As he was about to answer, I turned my head away from him, glanced at a passing grocery store, then closed my eyes and held my breath. I heard him say, "Some day, when you're older, I promise we'll talk."

His avoidance gave me temporary relief. Knowing the truth for certain would mean I'd have to grieve the illusion of my old identity. Dad seemed to intuitively sense that I wasn't ready or strong enough for that yet.

And then, as I continued to walk the dog, I remembered what happened two years later . . .

I had already gone off to college and was moving on with my life. On this day, I was sitting on the bleachers in the gym, awaiting the arrival of Leo Buscaglia with anticipation. The arena was packed. I'll never forget how excited I was. Buscaglia, a motivational speaker who taught how to have loving relationships, was speaking at the college I attended. After seeing him on TV so many Sunday afternoons as a kid, I couldn't wait to finally see him in person. Now I had my chance.

My heart began to swell in my chest as Buscaglia stepped up to the podium. First, he expressed his appreciation for being there. Then, he lectured. His message was on love. His humor and humanness made this very serious topic hit close to home. The two-hour talk flew by quickly as he took my heart from laughter to tears and back again. I felt extraordinarily open and alive.

As I listened, a still, small voice spoke to me
from within,

"You, too, some day will have your own special
message to offer others on love."

A chill came over my body, from the top of my head to
my toes. I looked out into the audience and felt our
connection. My heart was wide open and full of love.

"It is your destiny," I heard the voice say.

Suddenly, the magic was gone. The voice of my self-
doubt harshly contradicted the loving tone of the other.
*But how? Me? I know nothing about relationships! Who
would listen to me?*

"Just wait and be patient. You will see,"
The voice said again.

With that, the audience began clapping, giving
Buscaglia a standing ovation. It was the end of his
speech. But I also received the applause. For a moment, I
was sure it was for me. On some level, I knew it was my
destiny. Buscaglia lifted his hand in the air in gratitude
and slightly bowed his head, humbly accepting his
standing ovation before he left the podium.

I strolled back to my dorm in awe. *WOW!* was all I
could think. My body was filled with energy. My heart
was open. I felt love flowing through me towards the
whole world. I also felt a connection deep and full within
myself. This moment was the only moment that
mattered. The sky was midnight blue, the air crisp, and
the stars bright. I barely remember how I got back to my
dorm room. I was intoxicated with delight.

As I opened the door and entered my dorm room, four
of my college friends were sitting lined up at the back of

the room on one of the beds. They nervously glanced at one another. Their silence spoke volumes of concern.

"Hey, what's up guys? Is there something wrong?" I asked.

They continued to look at each other, perhaps hoping they wouldn't have to be the one to answer me. Finally, my friend Karen spoke up, "We have something to tell you."

Afraid and angry now about their hesitancy, I emphatically asked, "Karen, what's up?"

"It's your dad."

"What?" My wide open heart was now filled with panic. I was afraid to ask for more information. But it followed.

"He died tonight of a massive heart attack."

"What?" I demanded. "You must be wrong! That can't be right. I just spoke with him last night and he was fine. He is fine!" I insisted.

Suddenly my heart began to ache. The intensity of the love I'd felt at the talk was now replaced by the intensity of pain I was experiencing. How could this be? I felt shocked, confused, deeply saddened, hurt, and afraid.

Then, one of my friends spoke to help me clear the fog. She gently looked me in the eyes and reaffirmed the truth by saying, "Mary, your dad's wife, called and told us. It is true. We're so sorry."

As I remembered hearing the awful news, I recalled that, for some reason, I couldn't cry. Looking back today, I'm sure it was because the truth was too painful to endure. My heart felt broken. Being connected with myself in such a moment was difficult, since I'd been conditioned to do otherwise.

As I finished walking the dog, my eyes were filled with tears. I wondered, *Why is it so difficult for us to allow ourselves to feel?* And then I knew . . . For me, it was hopelessness and grief that felt overwhelming, and so I avoided them. Most of the people I knew were similarly conditioned either to "pull up their bootstraps" or to freeze up and try to "let stuff roll off their backs," as I had been doing in my marriage and career.

I also couldn't help but wonder, *Maybe most of us fear the feelings of being alive and passionate equally as much as we fear grief? Do we fear that if we open our hearts to joy and love we'll be vulnerable and exposed to pain too?*

There had been many occasions upon which I'd congratulated people for the wonderful things that happened in their lives. Now I could understand the fear I heard behind their comments when they would quickly say, "Thanks, but you know . . . tomorrow the other shoe could drop!"

Because my heart was so open to love after Leo Buscaglia's talk on the night that my dad passed away, I was emotionally wounded by the devastating news of his death. I reflected on all the detours I subsequently took to avoid connecting to my inner self: job performance, busyness, relationships, obsessing about the future, grandiose goals, and so on. I'd been dismissing my emotions and overcompensating with outer appearances and achievement.

Thinking about these tendencies made me realize I wasn't alone. Although my pain originated from its own unique story, I knew that many of the people whom I saw rushing around at work and in my neighborhood every day had their own painful stories too. They were all working hard, like me, to try to cover up their pain. I knew this because whenever I had risked sharing my story and pain with some of them, they were right there matching me with the same level of vulnerability.

Was there another option to living a fast-paced life of performance? How might I live a more meaningful and fulfilling life instead? Would I be able to help others answer these questions for themselves? Surely I was about to find out.

The Second Secret:
Embrace the Unknown

You don't have
All the answers,
So stop
Pretending you do.

Instead . . .
ASK:
"How might I . . . ?"

4

The Courage to Surrender the Need to Know

Dad's death had a strong effect on me. It wasn't just the loss of his life that was hard, it was also the fear that I'd lost the opportunity ever to find out the answer to the question, "Are you my biological father?" Knowing the answer to this question would give me truth. Not just about my parentage, but the truth that I could actually trust my instincts. Being able to trust my gut instinct would have given me the ability to make better decisions in all areas of my life. Instead, I doubted myself and quickly dismissed these hunches when they appeared without evidence. At that point, I didn't know how to trust.

Being in the unknown was difficult, and I didn't know any techniques yet that would change that reality. I knew I wasn't alone with my dilemma, because when I trained and coached people over the last few years in the corporate world I could see that others also struggled when they didn't have important answers. My mission as a corporate trainer was to empower individuals and company leaders to become more effective in their business and personal lives. I encouraged them to stay open and be patient, often advising my clients, "If you surrender your need to know, the answer will come to you in perfect timing." But it felt different when it was my life, my emotions, and my strong desire to know.

Hmm, it made me wonder. *Is this why the business world suggests leaving emotions at home?* It was clear that emotions could be a terrible distraction from the routines of life, yet disconnecting from emotions all together seemed to make things worse.

As I began to surrender my need to know on my timeline, I was consumed by feelings of fear, loss, and shame. Fear . . . that I would never know. Loss . . . of my hope to know. Shame . . . that I might have missed the opportunity to find out the truth that day in the truck with my dad when I was 16 years old.

Gradually, curiosity began to replace the agony of my grief. My heart opened and I stopped gripping so tightly to my need to know. My questions evolved. Soon, I began noticing, *Isn't that interesting. Dad has died. How might I find out if he was my real father now? And if he wasn't, how will I find out who my birth father was?*

The obvious person to ask would be my mother. But I had tried asking her for years when my gut told me that the man that raised me was not my real father. I knew if I asked her again, all I would hear was, "You and your silly imagination!" It was clear to me that I needed to find out another way. But how?

The more I surrendered and let go, the more my subconscious mind worked to find the answer for me. As a result, I was worrying less about the answer and simply getting on with my life.

My mornings were consumed with the training programs I would teach at companies on communication, conflict resolution, and problem solving. Teaching people how to surrender anxiety and worry, while they were waiting for answers, was a new aspect to my programs. As I was learning how to do this, I was teaching it too. My job always seemed to be the easiest place for me to apply and learn new lessons. Looking back, this was probably because my parents affirmed my competence when I was younger and gave me a lot of freedom to discover my own heart's desire in that area of my life.

Life was feeling full, and manageable. Gary was still traveling to Florida frequently. The kids were now in pre-school and elementary school. I felt fortunate that most of my programs were in the mornings so that I could pick up Alex at noon when pre-school was over and be home for Lisa after school. It felt like the best of both worlds: working and being an available mom. In the afternoons, Alex would nap and I was able to get my paperwork and phone calls done from my home office. Occasionally a cleaning lady would help me with the house. My mother would watch the kids here and there, and sometimes cook us a big meal.

Of course, as is always true, when we surrender our need to know, we receive the answer at the perfect time . . . when we're ready. This is always when we've given up fear and replaced it with trust and love.

After my feelings shifted from anxiety to positive expectancy, a cue regarding my birth father began coming to me in the form of a recurring dream, which always began with me going about my daily routine. In the first dream, I was grocery shopping at the local neighborhood store. I was pushing my grocery cart up and down the aisles, picking food off the shelves. Then, as I approached the last aisle, I turned the corner expecting to see what I always saw: the dairy section. Instead, to my surprise, I saw my mother sitting intimately with a strange man on old-fashioned ice cream chairs at a small, round table at the other end of the aisle.

The sudden sight shocked me. My mother and the man both looked odd and out of place engaged in their admiration of each other, as they gazed into each other's eyes, right in the middle of the grocery aisle. I could hardly bear looking at Mom. She looked desperate, attached, and entrenched. My heart began to race in panic, wanting to stop her from her public exposure of neediness. As I turned to see the man she was with, I woke up.

The next night, my dream was similar, except this time I was at home routinely vacuuming the living room of the house I lived in as a preschooler. One element remained the same: with the turn of a corner, I felt surprised and panicky. My mother was there again, clinging, clutching, and weeping, acting desperate, attached, and entrenched while holding hands with an unknown man. They were sitting at a round table together. And, as I turned to see his face, I woke up with my heart pounding to the point that I feared it would burst.

I wasn't clear what the dreams meant, so I decided to go to someone who could help me figure out what they were trying to tell me. That seemed like the responsible thing to do. Her name was Ingrid. She had a warm, non-threatening appearance, soft and comfortable. It felt like I was just chatting with an old friend when I talked with her. Her demeanor put me at ease. She was wise, but never made me feel like she was above me. Instead, it felt more like she was always in step with me, mirroring what my soul was crying out to say.

Ingrid was the pastor's wife. We'd met each other at the non-denominational Christian church I attended. She was also a counselor to whom I had spoken regarding my marital issues in the past. What impressed me most about her was just her way of being. I vividly remember her behavior one afternoon when she was hosting a going-away party at her home for one of our mutual bible study friends. Although she had one of the nicest homes in a brand-new subdivision near church, she was non-pretentious and real. That day, I grew in deep respect and fondness for Ingrid. There was a comfort she seemed to possess being in her own skin that I so wanted in my own life.

Now, two years later, when dreams haunted me night after night, there was no doubt that I would call her. Thus, I found myself in her office once again.

"So what can I help you with?" she asked me from her powder blue chair. I felt my body trembling, as I was trying so hard to contain my energy. It felt strange and embarrassing. *Where can I start? How can I explain all of this to Ingrid?* I wondered.

"Well I'm having these dreams that are repeated," I said. "Pretty much the same dreams, night after night. The details just change a bit. They're waking me up and I can't go back to sleep."

I could see Ingrid studying me while I was talking. She was watching my hands, which I was swinging in the air as if to slap my frustration and exhaustion away. She gazed at my cheeks and chin, now broken out in a pimply rash. As she took me in, I felt my anxiety exposed. A strong flush came onto my face. With my blonde hair, blue eyes, and fair complexion, the slightest embarrassment was always hard for me to hide.

I started to doubt whether I should be there. It felt bizarre to speak about my dream. *Could anyone be accurate in an interpretation of a dream?* I wondered. *How can I trust her input?* I debated my decision to share this vulnerable experience.

Ingrid leaned slightly forward in her chair and looked me deeply in the eyes, penetrating my heart. Her plain, almost nondescript features helped me to see beyond her exterior to her caring spirit. I began to trust again. "Would you describe the dream to me?" she said softly, as if she knew she was pulling me back into reality. Her sandy blonde hair framed a warm expression. Then, she sat patiently, waiting and interested.

"Sure," I said. "The dreams start out with me just doing my thing: grocery shopping, vacuuming, or whatever." As I began to describe the dreams, I felt my body re-experiencing the details. My breath was staccato. My heart was pounding louder. And my face was flushed. "At first, I'm feeling at peace. Then, suddenly, I turn a corner and there she is. She's always at a round table, holding a man's hand. They look intensely involved."

"Who is 'she'?" Ingrid inquired.

"My mom."

She paused. With a gentle glance, she looked over at me and softly asked, "What does the man look like?"

"I don't know," I replied, feeling frustrated and flushing all over my body. "That's when I always wake up." I felt like a failure: stuck and powerless. Although I was sure that deep down inside I knew the truth, for some reason I couldn't cross the hurdle I must in order to face what I needed to know.

Ingrid didn't allow me to continue to feel hopeless for long. She interrupted me and asked in a hopeful voice, "May we try something?"

She waited for my nod of approval, and then continued. "Great. Close your eyes. Try going back into the dream at the grocery store." I followed her instructions. "Walk down the aisle and do your shopping. This time, I want you to prepare yourself and expect your mom around the corner . . . Now, take a slow, deep breath. Turn the corner. What do you see?"

"Just my mom," I replied, disappointed that I was still blocked from being able to see the truth.

"Okay. Look at her and take another deep breath. This time feel your body's reaction. Tell me, what are you feeling toward your mom?"

"Anger." I could feel the intensity of it swelling up inside of me. But my body wanted to hold all that energy within. I was starting to stiffen up. My teeth were clenched and my jaw had tightened. As my awareness of my body grew, I could feel my shoulder and neck tightening as well. My heart started to race. I looked over at Ingrid again. "I feel rage."

She nodded to affirm my reaction. "What are you feeling right now towards the man?" she asked.

I could feel the energy in my body change. The tightness disappeared. My shoulders went limp. My breathing became longer and deeper. My eyes started to well up with tears. "I feel hurt, neglected and unimportant," I said, as I looked down into my lap with shame.

"Close your eyes again and tell me more. Now, take another deep breath." She patiently waited until I was done. "Stay there at the corner. Look over at them again. What is the hurt about?"

The silence following her question illuminated the answer that hid within me. I understood it so clearly now. "He wants her, but not me." I said, opening my eyes to look directly at her. "I almost feel jealous." Then, I had another insight. "Wow . . . this is interesting," I told her. "I've had similar dreams regarding my husband and other women. The same feelings of hurt and jealousy are in those dreams too."

Ingrid nodded as if she wasn't surprised. Although she acknowledged what I said, she continued to stay focused on the original dream. "Okay, close your eyes again. Now try to picture your mom with the man. What do you see?"

"I think he has dark hair," I said, somewhat reluctantly. She was patient as I continued to try to see the man. Then he started to become clearer to me. "Actually, he sort of looks like my brother." I opened my eyes again and leaned forward. "Maybe this is about somebody taking my brother away." I was trying to rationalize a very odd experience.

Ingrid didn't buy into my half-hearted explanation. She knew that being in the unknown for a while without an explanation was hard for me. I knew that too. *How could anyone ever figure out the real meaning of this dream?* I wondered. Guessing wasn't good enough for me. I needed to know.

My self-doubt didn't create a flinch in Ingrid. The room was still. She didn't move. She just looked at me and waited until I settled in my seat again. I could feel the heat in my body return. This time it felt neither like hurt nor like angry energy. It was heavy. I looked over at her, sensing she had something to say.

"Didn't you once mention to me that there was some question regarding your birth father?"

I was surprised. When had I told her? It was something I rarely mentioned. I never felt comfortable talking to anyone about my hunch. "I don't remember telling you that, but, yes, I have always wondered," I said in amazement.

"Well, I think you need to pursue the answer to that question, unless you want to continue having those dreams that wake you up every night," she said.

5

The Courage to
Let Go of the Outcome

As weeks passed, I struggled with what to do. The suspicion that my dad was not my biological father was still nagging at me. But I was an adult now, and I knew that I needed to make a different choice this time. Instead of running to my mom for validation of my suspicions, I needed to get grounded. To settle my thoughts and feelings, I decided to spend more time in quiet self-reflection. Many activities helped me to do this: exercising, cleaning the house, cutting the grass, walking the dog, meditating, taking hot baths, reading the Bible, and journaling. I used anything where I could still my mind and enter a state of connection with my surroundings and self.

Due to my uncertainty, I didn't talk much about my dreams and suspicions with other people, including my husband. On the rare occasions when I would bring up the fact that I wondered about my birth father and the meaning of the dreams, he had little to say. I didn't fault him for that. This was an experience with which he couldn't identify. Yet, I often felt sad and alone.

Just about the time I admitted my need to create a connection with others around this issue, my friend Jack from church called. We were on a committee together. As we began to talk, he noticed I was heavy-hearted. I didn't have the courage to tell him what I was facing, however, because the old, skeptical message of "you and your overactive imagination" was creeping up on me and holding me hostage from my truth. Although I remember wanting to say something, I didn't know how to blurt out my dilemma.

Then, something strange happened. Jack communicated what he was facing in his personal life. He'd recently found out that he was illegitimate and was struggling with whether or not to contact his birth father. I was shocked by the similarity to my issue. Even more amazingly, by sharing his story unsolicited, he unblocked my doubt about my need to look into the truth regarding my parentage.

Now, I felt hopeful. I knew there was a chance that I too could find out about my birth father. Suddenly, I felt unstuck, trusting instead that finding evidence could be possible. Like me, he was surprised as I shared with him what I was going through. It comforted him too.

I began to cry on the phone in relief that someone understood my confusion. I felt the courage to explore my question, as I embraced and released feelings I'd dismissed for so long. By the time I hung up the phone, I felt at peace once again.

After the phone conversation, I couldn't help considering, *Is it possible for us to simply ask, be still, and let the answer come to us?* In order to make a shift, I would have to confront and relinquish several beliefs. This would help me to be in a more trusting mode to receive what was needed. First, I would have to die to the belief "If it were meant to be, it's up to me!" In my new realm of experience, I didn't always have to be the doer. I would have to learn to surrender situations and to ask and stay open. In being with situations differently, I would be able to trust that my needs would be met appropriately, even though I wouldn't be the one in control. Interestingly, I found I would also have to give up my belief that I had a time limit. I discovered that I felt pressured and anxious, partly because I thought I might run out of time to find an answer.

I was ready to try another way. Was it part of my unique gifts as a woman to model the ability to attract and receive versus "just doing it?" Perhaps this ability was what was needed to balance the busyness of our chaotic, fast-paced, and action-packed world. I was beginning to feel a purpose for my life. Were all of these experiences happening so that I could learn the lesson of trusting and allowing and, perhaps, then teach this process to others? My curiosity gave me the courage to explore a new way of being with uncertainty.

To learn to let go of my tendency to want to control, I needed to learn how to relax. One of the places in which I found the most solitude was the master bathroom that Gary and I had just remodeled. Its Jacuzzi whirlpool bath with hot bubbles, music softly playing in the background, and sunlight beaming onto an earth-toned marble deck became an environment that comforted my soul. It was a place I could go to feel peaceful, quiet, and still. In this space, I became ready to connect with my feeling of powerlessness, so that I could finally surrender and ask, "What are the dreams trying to tell me?"

In order to attract truth, part of my development was to explore deeper aspects of my heart. I had to learn to be curious about any emotions and beliefs that were getting in the way of trusting that the answer could come to me if I simply asked. Exploring, embracing, and releasing any fears around the outcome was part of this journey.

As I experienced my own anxiety and hopelessness at times, I realized that this state of being closed me off to possibilities. As I awakened to this awareness, I saw another option. Instead of feeling anxious or depressed, I could embrace feelings that were hidden from me for so long. There, waiting to be acknowledged and released, were my feelings of sadness and powerlessness.

As I was learning to be in the unknown, I was letting go of my need to have my answers immediately. Because of this, I was more able to get on with my life. However, my husband and I were becoming estranged. I was never quite sure of the reasons. Maybe he thought I was acting a bit strange. Intimate questions and conversations were difficult. They brought up a lot of shame in both of us.

My perception was that Gary was becoming bitter and angry toward me because I was no longer the strong and capable producer that I'd been when he met me. In actuality, the distance between us was probably the product of my internal struggle to shift my sense of reality more than of anyone else's struggle. I needed to know: Am I enough, just for being who I am?

Until this point, many of my actions had usually been chosen to make a good impression on other people and not ruffle their feathers. As I began taking my own needs and feelings into consideration when I made decisions, a big gap appeared in my relationship with my husband. My choices were new for both of us. We were both being pushed out of our comfort zones. While this gave us an opportunity, it was also a fork in the road: we could either dive more deeply into our own insecurities, thus gaining wisdom; or we could stay at the surface and be angry at each other. Unfortunately, we couldn't seem to get past the wall of our anger.

Although Gary's counselor and the members of his men's group suggested that he give our relationship time to develop into something new, he began expressing a desire to get a divorce. Due to my own fears of being controlled and of not being loved, I couldn't help but hear that as a threat: "Change back to who you were, or else!"

While that was going on at home, my job continued to be a refuge for me. It was easy for me to connect with my clients and be supportive of everything they were going through. I examined the difference in how I related in these two environments. At work, I gave myself the freedom of being in touch with my emotions and open to the unknown. I trusted that I'd receive the answers I needed. Because I was more real and vulnerable, others would mirror these qualities back to me. With equal openness, my clients often shared their feelings of being overwhelmed and anxious about the many unknowns and changes at work. I understood how chaos made them feel. Although my scenario was different, my response to it was basically the same.

Coaching my clients on facing uncertainty, I could hear myself in their comments and see why I was stuck at home. My fear and anxiety were closing me off from receiving the truth about my birth father. This awareness led me to have a permanent emotional shift. One day, as I embraced my feelings of sadness and powerlessness, I heard a voice in my head say, "Call Mary."

Mary was my dad's second wife. They'd married when I was nine years old. It had been many years since I'd spoken with her. What would I say? What if it wasn't true? Then I'd really feel silly. For several days, I couldn't get up enough courage to call.

The good news was that, this time, I didn't dismiss my feelings when anxiety overcame me. Instead, I allowed myself to become aware of it, and to be open and honest with myself, while I considered all the possibilities. Rather than looking at my choices either as completely letting go, trusting, and allowing, or as completely taking control, I posed a new kind of question: "How might I go about finding the answer in a way that is comfortable for me?" Even though I knew I could call and ask Mary for her help, I stayed open to every other possible way to find the answer. Who else might know?

My first thought was to go to my obstetrician. He was a family friend as well as the doctor who'd delivered my brother, both of my girls, and me. I felt a special affinity with him because of the way he opened his heart to me whenever I saw him. When he asked how I was, it was clear he was really interested, not just being casually friendly. Wondering how I might find out about my birth father, his caring face came to mind.

So, a week later, I went to his office. My throat began

to swell as I told him my doubts about my birth father. "Do you know?" I asked him.

"For legal reasons, regarding medical privacy, I can't say too much. But I can tell you this: Your blood type is rare. You are AB negative. Only 3 percent of the people in the United States have that blood type. Your mother's blood type is positive. Therefore, if you can find out your father's blood type, you will know. Your birth father has to be a negative blood type."

Although this information did not give me the complete answer, I felt hopeful. It gave me a direction and a possible way to find out the truth. So I tried digging up medical records, but my dad didn't seem to have any that showed his blood type. He'd never had surgery.

Finally, I recognized that I was doing everything I could to avoid calling Mary. As I became honest with myself, I realized that my feelings of fear and shame were controlling me and keeping me from doing what I needed to do. *Will Mary think I am ridiculous for asking this embarrassing question?* Just by recognizing my fear, I could more easily release it. As I embraced my fear, I found my courage, and I called.

"Hi Mary," I said in a nervous and heavy voice. "This is Susie."

Mary was hesitant. I could tell that she knew this was not just a casual call. My voice immediately began to shake.

"I have a strange favor to ask you. I don't know if Dad ever said anything to you, but I've suspected for a long time that I may not be his birth child." I paused and waited to hear her response. This was different from the experience I'd had in the car with my father. This time I really wanted to know. Not knowing would be worse. I heard her take a deep breath.

Again, I asked, "Did Dad ever mention that possibility to you?"

She hesitated, and then asked, "Do you really want to know?"

Tears flowed down my cheeks. She'd already confirmed my gut feeling. She stayed on the phone with me as I cried for several minutes. As I sobbed, I let go of the outcome and faced the fear, loss, and shame I'd been holding onto for years. I'd blocked these feelings for so long because I'd been afraid that the truth would hurt more than I could bear. I was full of fear about the losses I'd have to experience, including the loss of my identity, as I knew it, and the loss of my relatives who were no longer related. There was also so much shame in not knowing to whom I really belonged.

After I regained my composure, Mary went on to explain. She said exactly what I needed to hear at the time. "You know how much your dad loved you. Whether or not he was your biological father, he always saw himself as your dad. He mentioned to me one time that he wondered, but he didn't know for sure."

Her compassion brought comfort to my pain. I thanked her and expressed my gratitude for her openness. Not much else was said.

In the days that followed, I felt like I had no option other than to surrender to the unknown. I used the situation as an opportunity to practice embracing my feelings. Gradually, a sense of peace replaced my anxiety. I began to trust that I would receive the answers I needed in perfect timing. My heart's desire was for some evidence.

As I was learning to connect with my heart and let go of controlling the outcome, life was taking care of the details. Within weeks, the phone rang. It was Mary. "Guess what?" She asked with deep satisfaction. "I found an old donor's card your father had from the one time he gave blood."

"You're kidding!" I was amazed that she would still have such information 16 years after the fact. In

partial disbelief, I asked, "What made you keep
something like that?"

"I don't know. It was in a pile of papers your dad kept
in a little black box. I just felt like I wasn't supposed to
throw it away. I happened to be looking through some
old things the other day and ran across it. I thought it
might be helpful in order for you to find out for sure if he
was your birth father."

I felt both elated and nervous. My biggest fear was
that I was wrong. Yet, I needed to know immediately
what the donor card said. The possibility of grieving the
loss of my identity didn't compare to facing down the
shaming voice that for years told me I'd been imagining
this. So I asked, "Mary, does it show a blood type?"

"Yes. It's O positive."

My stomach felt like it went from a knot to suddenly
being untied and loose. "Are you absolutely sure?"

"Yes."

I felt as though a heavy cloak had been lifted off my
body. Feelings of freedom and nakedness came over me
all at once. In part, it felt awesome. In another way, I
felt a bit raw and exposed. I was amazed at my
immediate transformation.

What does this mean for me? I wondered. Gratitude
quickly became my predominant feeling. I'd just
received the confirmation I was waiting for! My blood
was AB negative. My mom's was positive and so was
Dad's. Those facts proved he wasn't my birth father,
according to my doctor. I felt tremendous relief to receive
confirmation that I'd known the truth all along. It wasn't
my "crazy imagination." It was my intuitive knowing.
With this awareness, I now understood the bigger
concern that had been haunting me for years: Could I
trust myself? It was healing to know I could.

Then, Dad's face came vividly to mind. I remembered
when we were in his truck driving down the street. It was
as though we were together again and he was saying, "I

promised you that some day, when you were older, we would talk." Warmth came over me as I experienced the power of our oneness firsthand.

I shared my memory with Mary.

"What are you going to do now?" she asked.

"I don't know," I said, wondering the same thing myself. I hesitated before getting off the phone.

Internally, I was thinking, *Am I satisfied?* Curiosity began to run through my body. *Who is my father, then?* The question brought only a blank white screen into my mind's eye. Dissatisfaction settled on my shoulders like a heavy, limp blanket.

Suddenly, I knew what I needed to do. I turned to Mary for support, "No, that's wrong; I do know! I need to find out who my real father is. I just don't know how I'm going to do that yet."

Although my recurring dreams stopped once I found out the truth about Dad, I still couldn't help but spend time wondering, *Who am I?* So I brought the question to therapy.

Ingrid had suggested I read stories about Jesus from the Bible. She thought they would give me strength . . . not in the traditional sense of reading and memorizing scripture, but instead by identifying my pain with His. Her hope was that I would not feel so alone. She was correct. The stories helped me fight off my feelings of fear, loss, and shame. Through them, I realized that deception and betrayal were more about the condition of the human heart and less about me. I stopped taking my birth situation and the secret so personally. Consequently, I could surrender my attachment to a specific outcome and I was able to desire the truth no matter what.

Often, to quiet my mind, I would get a massage. Although it had been a while since I'd seen Michele, my favorite local massage therapist, I decided it was time to make an appointment.

"Hi," she said, smiling at me warmly. "What do you need today?"

I looked at her and said, "Today I'm here for some deep grief work. My emotions have been taking quite a toll on my body. I need the massage for relaxation, and as a means of centering, so that I'm open for some big events that lie ahead for me. I can sense that I need to release a lot of sadness."

Michele stepped outside of the room as I took off my clothes and got under a warm sheet. The room smelled like fresh berries. I looked around while I waited for her to come in. A knick-knack on her shelf caught my attention. Engraved on it was the phrase: When God closes a door, he opens a window. I felt a sense of peace from that promise. I knew it would be true for me–in God's time. Lying on my back on the massage table, I heard three soft knocks on the door.

"Come in," I said, letting her know I was ready.

She circled around the table and, as she did, she gently squeezed my foot in a nurturing way. Then she began the day's healing. The entire time on the table, I prayed. I sensed I was not praying alone.

"Lord, heal my heart. Fill me with Your love." Those were the words that kept coming to me.

I meditated on God's love and healing powers while Michele's fingers started to flow like wind through my hair, parting it several times with each stroke of each finger. The rhythm moved faster and faster until she squeezed my hair in her hands. I felt a slight pang, as though I could feel her squeezing out all of my negative thoughts and emotions.

Next, she gently lifted up the sheet and tucked it in, ensuring that it covered my breasts. Then, she began to concentrate on massaging my heart area. Her hands seemed to begin to melt into my chest. I saw a picture in my mind's eye of the Lord's hands replacing hers. It felt safe, loving and healing.

My mind shifted to my mother and I began to feel my throat choke up. My eyes swelled. I remembered how much I had longed for her to be emotionally present so that she could nurture me. But that comfort wasn't available from my mom. Not because she didn't love me, but because she didn't have it inside to give. I remembered times when she stayed up all night drinking and worrying. There were other nights she promised to be home, but didn't get in until after I was asleep. And the times she was around and not drinking, she often was so self-absorbed that I still felt lonely. As I connected with my pain and longing, wisdom came to me. My loneliness, sadness, and shame made sense to me now. With each deep breath, I released the pain and took in all the love I needed. I remembered my dream . . . Mom was busy looking for love outside of herself; that's where all of her energy had gone. She'd never learned how to tap into the wealth of love available to her within herself.

I started to sob almost uncontrollably. But I didn't feel embarrassed. I felt alone in the room, yet so deeply connected that there was no room for my aloneness anymore. As Michele continued to massage the area, I saw the Lord taking my heart and placing it in His hand like a piece of clay–rotating it, re-forming it, and molding it to His desire, and then doing it all over again. Michele's hands became the potter's wheel.

After several minutes of this, she moved her hands to spread my shoulders apart. It was as if she was widening the space so that my healing heart had room to expand. It felt as if her movements were divinely orchestrated.

"I'll be back in a few minutes. Take your time getting up," Michele said as she finished her last sweeping strokes nearly 30 minutes later.

I did just what she recommended; yet, I still felt lightheaded as I sat up on the table. Slowly, I got dressed. I could feel the silk undergarments against my skin as I put them on. *Strange,* I thought, *I've done this a million times before and never noticed how wonderful the fabric truly felt.* I felt feminine . . . as pretty as silk.

After I was dressed and seated by her desk, Michele returned. She brought me a cool glass of water.

"Do you ever pray over your clients when you massage?" I asked.

"In fact, I do–sometimes more than others. It just depends on whether or not I feel moved to do so."

"I bet you did a lot today, didn't you?"

She smiled, as if I had given her confirmation that God indeed was using her.

"Yes, I did. The whole time," she said.

I smiled back at her, as tears flowed to my eyes once more. "Thank you. You made a difference."

It didn't take long after the massage that I knew what to do next. "Call your brother," I heard the still, small voice gently guide me. "He has a way to communicate with your mom that you don't. He will support you."

My brother Gary is 11 months and 3 weeks older than I am. We always thought it was fun that we were the same age for one week each year. I was proud to have him as my big brother. He was the star athlete in high school and everyone in the city knew him. The girls knew him because of his charming personality and good looks, and the guys knew him because he was one of the best all-round athletes in the state. Although he had a big, athletic appearance, he also had a soft heart like a teddy bear.

I thought about the time when I was six years old and he was seven. He'd saved up all of his money to buy me a teddy bear for my birthday. The sparkle in his eye as he gave it to me was something I still remember today.

Calling him to tell him what I knew about Dad was very hard. My brother always held a special place in my heart and I was afraid that this news could mean he was only my half-brother. *Would that change our relationship?*

Resisting this new fear, I took a deep breath and

found my courage. Once I did, I dialed his number. As the phone rang, I could feel my heart beating faster. I wondered, *Will this make sense to him or will he think I am crazy?*

The third ring was interrupted by a strong, "Hello."

"Hi, it's me. Did I interrupt you from something?"

My voice was shaking a bit. I wondered if I was catching him in the right state of mind for such a heavy blow. My brother was a salesperson and a district manager for a chemical company. He used his home as his office. It was about 4:30 p.m. and I wanted to catch him alone before his wife came home.

"No, this time is okay. What's up?"

Words would not flow. What could I say? I started to get choked up. Finally, I said, "I have a favor to ask you. I don't know where to start. I'm feeling really awkward right now." At this point, I was fighting to keep the tears back. They were stuck in my throat, ready to burst it open. "I recently found out that Dad is not my real father. I'm so upset, and I need to talk to Mom about who is my real birth father . . . But I'm afraid to talk to her about this. I thought maybe you could help."

There was nothing I could do then to hold back the tears. They came flooding out of the gate. It felt so good to let my grief out. My brother had never really heard me cry like that before. I was emotional as a kid, but not a crier. Expressing sadness was foreign to my family.

"Are you sure?" he asked in surprise.

"Yes, I am sure."

"How do you know this?"

"By our blood types. I happen to have AB negative. Mom's blood type is positive and so is Dad's. My birth father has to be negative."

As I told him the entire story, I could feel how it was affecting him too.

"Gee, I wonder what blood type I have?" he said in a deep reflective tone.

"I don't know, but it's not hard to find out if you really want to know."

"Well, let's deal with you first," he said in an abrupt tone of voice.

"Thanks," I said. "I know this is going to be hard for you too. You and Mom have always had a tight relationship, and now I'm asking you to be here for me even though it might upset her. I just want you to know that I realize it won't be easy."

In a firm, loving voice he said, "I do what I think is right. You have a right to know who you are." We both paused to take in his words. Moments later he broke the silence, but this time his tone had softened.

"You know, it's kind of strange . . ."

"What?" I asked

"Just the other day, I happened to turn on 'Oprah' in the background as I was finishing my paperwork. She was talking about this very subject. Oprah's show was about kids who didn't know who their real birth parents were. The kids were adults now, and they spoke about how it still bothered them. A few of them said that somehow they knew, but that it was hidden from them for years. Once they found out, it was a big relief. So, I understand why you need to know. You have a right to know."

I was amazed. What if he hadn't watched "Oprah" that day? What were the chances that the message would've reached him? Would he still have had the same empathy for my predicament? I felt deeply grateful. This time, my tears flowed to express my relief and gratitude. As we ended the conversation, he reassured me that he would contact Mom and see about setting up a time for us all to get together.

Weeks passed before my brother Gary and I spoke again. He'd contacted our mother and tried to set up a time for us all to meet, but she'd kept putting him off saying she was busy.

Waiting in the unknown was still difficult for me, however I was learning that patience was part of being in the process of connecting within and with others. So, finally, we met, weeks later at her house. Mom looked puzzled, as she answered the door, wondering why we were both there.

We all sat down in the living room and my brother started, "Mom, this isn't going to be easy, so I'm just going to say it." He had a firm, loving voice.

I looked over at my mom as he told her that I'd discovered I had a different birth father than Dad. She was silent. She didn't respond to him. Instead, she just sat there.

I so desperately wanted to hear something from her, yet all I could feel was the emotional shift in the room as she avoided his declaration. I began to feel my powerlessness as I could see my mom struggling to find her power. Her back became stiff, as she held her breath so that none of her emotions would give us a clue. In that instant, I realized it wasn't going to be easy to persuade her to speak honestly about her past. I wanted to know who my father was and why she'd kept this a secret.

Mom didn't offer any comment on my news other than to say she needed to think about everything we'd said. Her body was stoic and her face blank as she stood up from the white couch, motioning for us to leave. As she walked us to the door, I felt about 16 years old again. I was well aware of feeling the same powerless, lonely feeling I'd often felt at that age when my mother wouldn't give me what I needed. She looked over and glared at me with such a burning stare that words weren't necessary to express her feelings. Her energy demanded, "How dare you do this to me?"

Weeks passed and we never heard more on the subject. Waiting was extremely hard.

Why was it so hard for me to sit in the waiting room

of life? I knew I wasn't alone, that this type of experience is difficult for most people. Yet, some people are fortunate enough to see in hindsight that their waiting time didn't go wasted. Sometimes "waiting time" is actually an important incubation period, necessary for gaining new insights. However, that wasn't making it easier.

During my waiting time, the biggest change that occurred in me was my view of my mother. A new perception emerged. My inward connection helped me to see her from a more human perspective. I was gradually able to let go of seeing her as a powerful woman who held the key to my identity. Instead, I began to see her as someone who shared many of the same fears I did. Just because she was older and an authority figure didn't mean she didn't have struggles too.

Developing this awareness gave me even more confidence in the power of my self-connection. There was great wisdom available that it would enable me not only to learn about who I was, it would also help me to perceive what was going on with others. This new way of being allowed me to recognize that Mom was just as scared, lonely, and insecure as I was at times.

I now knew that her choice to withhold information and nurturing wasn't personal. She wasn't trying to withhold anything from me; she was simply defending her image and avoiding feeling her feelings. Although I didn't like her choice, understanding it helped reveal my own options within this very difficult situation. My biggest choice was to shift my perception of who had the power. I no longer believed she had the power to deceive, betray, or nurture me. I could now see the truth: I chose to deceive, betray, and abandon myself because of my own fears. Deep inside truth and love were always there for me, when I was ready to explore and embrace it. Until I was ready to take responsibility, I had blamed her for my own self-deception and fear. Following this insight, I felt empathy and compassion.

As I moved from fear to love and from sympathy to compassion, my heart opened. Suddenly I could see all kinds of possibilities. Soon, I felt ready to take another step.

As I waited for my mom to contact me, I was getting on with the other aspects of my life. I felt more connected to the people with whom I interacted, because I could identify more with their experiences. I couldn't believe the similarities! So many of the complaints I heard both from my friends and from those I trained in the workplace were the same. The complaints often revolved around feelings of betrayal, rejection, or the fear of being deceived. When people would share their personal stories with me, I noticed that they usually described themselves as victims. It seemed to be an easier and more preferred way of seeing things than taking responsibility. I could understand why, as I had the same habit of framing situations that way too at times.

I wondered, *What would happen if everybody realized that our problems aren't all derived from other people's behavior–that problems are always self-created on an underlying level? What would that mean in terms of accepting this powerless feeling inside?*

Asking, *What do I need to learn here?* was quite helpful. So was asking, *What is my responsibility in this?* And, *What is real and true?*

6

The Courage to Ask
the Difficult Questions

I knew what I had to do. So, one afternoon, I called my brother. We agreed we'd go over to my mother's house again and tell her that she couldn't delay the conversation about my birth father any longer. That very night my brother, his wife, my husband, and I knocked on Mom's door. She seemed surprised at our persistence. I'm sure she was convinced that her avoidance had made us lose our focus. But it hadn't.

There we were, sitting on the couch at her house once again. The room was silent, as she glared at me in the same way she had before we left the last time. This time felt different though. My response to her behavior had shifted. She could feel that it no longer had the same effect on me. I looked deep into her eyes, hoping to transmit feelings of compassion and love to her instead of fear and shame. I communicated with her non-verbally, as best I could, and told her through my eyes and the power of an open heart that I understood her fear. I looked deeply and tenderly into her eyes to reassure her that I was not trying to harm her. I just needed to know: Who am I? To whom do I belong? She softened, as though she heard me and understood.

I gently spoke, "Mom, we need to know the truth. We can't keep avoiding this issue."

Reaching out a hand, her eyes pleaded for me to sit next to her. By the tone in her voice and the look in her eyes, I sensed that part of her fear was the thought of being rejected.

"Mom, I just want to know the truth. I will not think badly of you," I assured her as I sat down beside her.

Following a deep breath, she began to tell her story. "I met him when I was in my early 20s. I was separated from your father at the time and looking for a job. He was the owner of a real estate company where I was hoping to work. We met several times over coffee and really hit it off. We fell in love."

She continued to explain with tears rolling down her cheeks, as though she were back in the moment 33 years earlier . . .

"We wanted to get married. Although we were both separated at the time, in the eyes of the Catholic Church we were still married to other people. The priest told us that if we got married we would be ex-communicated. I couldn't make that choice with our family being so devoutly Catholic. Grandma would never have spoken to me again. That day, we decided it was over. I'll never forget it . . . I cried as I walked out the priest's office, crunched up my Kleenex in a ball, and threw it in the garbage bin outside his door. That day was the end of it."

As she told her story, I could sense her deep sadness. What struck me the most was how their relationship ended. I wondered, *End of what?* I knew she was referring to the relationship, but I couldn't help but wonder if her broken relationship ended up being the end of her peace, passion, and fulfillment in life as well. Had she put so much stock in this relationship that the broken dream actually made her lose her connection with her heart and soul? Now I more clearly understood why she'd been inaccessible to me emotionally all these years and I hadn't received the nurturing I'd sought.

It was clear that she was telling the truth. Everything about what she was saying was congruent. Her words, her body language, and her tone of voice matched.

Then, unexpectedly, she turned to my brother and said, "As long as we've come this far, I need to tell you that you may be his son too."

My brother and I stared at each other with our

eyebrows up and jaws hanging down. Both of us were caught off guard. The room was silent for about 30 seconds and the air was thick until my brother got up off his seat. To break the tension, he became playful and, in a Jim Carey type of voice, announced, "All-righty then! Well . . . I guess it's Miller Time!"

The Third Secret:

Embrace Intuitive Wisdom

You asked . . .
Now, stay open to receive guidance.

SAY:
*"I AM able to attract truth and
wisdom in perfect timing"*

7

The Courage to Claim the Power of the Present Moment

Weeks passed after my mother's vulnerable exposure of her past. Although I was feeling mostly relieved to be living in the truth, my brother was struggling with the surprising, yet still ambiguous news. Although I could understand how horrible he felt being surprised like that, I was happy at the thought that he and I could still possibly be full brother and sister.

At this point, I became so curious about my birth father that I wanted to meet him and experience who he was by myself. My mother wasn't happy about the request to put us in touch. She had another plan. She wanted all of us to meet together at the same time. I reiterated that I wanted to see him alone first. After much consideration, she told me where he lived and how to reach him.

"Did you tell him that I confronted you on this?"

"Yes, I did." She answered.

Several weeks later I called him. It took me a while to get up the nerve, because I wasn't sure how he would respond. But soon my curiosity overpowered my fear of the outcome. It was a Saturday afternoon and I went to my office so that I would have privacy when I called him at home. I was still feeling a bit nervous as he answered the phone. His voice resonated throughout my body.

"Hello," he said in a gruff voice.

"Hi, is this Richard?" I asked.

"Yes."

"Hi. I understand that my mother told you I might call."

"Yes."

I could hear pots and pans banging in the background. I wondered, *Might that be his wife?* More so, I wondered if she suspected anything or knew. *Is it possible that she never had a clue that her husband strayed and had two children with another woman?* That kind of scary thought often made me feel vulnerable in my romantic relationships.

Because I didn't know the situation and I wanted to respect their relationship, I asked, "Is this a good time for you?"

"Not really," he said in a sharp and sarcastic tone.

"Would it be better if I called you Monday morning around 8:45 a.m. after my children are off to school?"

"That would be fine."

As I hung up I marveled, *Why does his voice sound so familiar?* Although I was looking forward to talking with him, I was feeling a bit uncomfortable with what appeared to be a secret he was keeping from his wife. Because I admitted to myself that I didn't know how to handle this situation, I was able to let go of control and ask my intuitive wisdom to be with me through the coming events.

That weekend passed quickly and Monday morning soon appeared. I hurried to get the kids off to school so I could call him exactly at 8:45 a.m., as I said I would. We had a short conversation focused on getting together. Not much was said except, "Hi. When should we meet?" "Where should we meet?" and, "What do you look like?"

Now, two weeks later, I was going to meet my birth father for the first time at age 33. I prayed with a friend on the phone for an hour before I had to leave my house. I asked the Lord to protect me, hold me in His truth, and provide me with the words I needed to say. I also asked my intuitive wisdom to be present with me, to keep me in the moment, and to help me let go of any need to control the outcome of our meeting. I was feeling a lot of fear about the unknown . . . Would I like him? Would he like me? Would it be awkward? What would we say to each other? After praying, I was still a bit nervous, but I felt more at peace.

My birth father Richard and I met in the lobby of the church that I attended. I arrived first and sat in the chairs near the entrance in the hope that I would recognize him. He'd described himself on the phone, "What do I look like? I'm about six-foot-two, with salt-and-pepper hair and dark eyes. I'll be wearing a black jacket and hat."

"Thank you. That will help," I said.

As he appeared in the lobby that morning, I did recognize him. Not because of his description, but because he had a familiar appearance. *What was it about him that seems so familiar?* I wondered.

Our eyes met. We recognized each other and greeted each other with a warm handshake and nervous eyes.

"Your mother didn't tell me you were so beautiful."

"Well, thank you," I said. I could truly receive his compliment because I felt beautiful that morning. Not so much because of the way I looked outwardly, but because I felt lovely on the inside. My heart was open and my motives were pure.

"You're quite charming," I responded. "I can see why my mother was drawn to you." I could sense that my truthfulness was uncomfortable for him.

He abruptly changed the tone and said, "So, what can I do for you? You know, this is a bit awkward for me."

"I know . . . for me too."

We just looked at each other. For moments, it was silent.

Then I said, "Thank you for coming today. I really wanted to meet you in person, alone. I don't know exactly why, but I did. I want to assure you that I respect your privacy and your relationship with your wife and family. What you do about this is your choice. I just wanted to get some answers to satisfy my curiosity."

"Well, I'm glad about that." He sighed. "I have to admit, I've been really nervous since your mother called me a few weeks ago out of the blue."

"I'm sure you were. It must have been hard to live with this secret all those years," I said respectfully, but honestly.

"I didn't know all these years, you know."

I looked closely at him as he said that. I felt that, at some level, he'd probably known the truth, but didn't want to believe it. I was convinced he'd tried to persuade himself of what he'd just told me. His face was pleading for me to believe him so that he could continue to live in a way he was comfortable–in denial.

Intuitively, I knew that neither one of us was going to change our perceptions, so I just let it go. I felt peaceful, since I could feel the breadth of my personal growth, and trusted in my own truth.

The conversation remained on the surface after that. Our jobs, likes, dislikes, health issues, and people we knew in common were among the topics that felt safe. I could sense a parallel dialogue at some other level that wasn't spoken in words. It was almost as if I could hear the true questions of our unconscious minds.

One of my unconscious questions was: *"Why did you stray from your wife and get involved with my mother?"* I looked deeply in his eyes as I wondered. Then the answer came to me in a still small voice: *"It was the passion."* My hunch was that he was leading a passionless life of rightly chosen decisions, comforts, and securities, yet one in which his heart wasn't open. He proudly mentioned that he was a Catholic and had five other children. He mentioned that his wife stayed at home. I wondered if he'd been looking for something exciting to fill a void.

Suddenly, our underlying conversation connected to our actual conversation, when he said, "Your mother was a lot of fun, but I don't think it would've lasted."

"Why?" I inquired.

"She was fun and also a little wild. That got to me after a while. I wasn't sure I wanted that lifestyle on a permanent basis." We touched hearts for a moment. That quality was what I found most endearing yet difficult about my mother too. After an hour's chat, Richard walked me to my car and we said good-bye.

"Your father must have been proud of you," he said.

"Yes, he was. I felt very loved by him."

He acknowledged my relationship with my dad with a smile on his face and a sparkle in his eye. As we said good-bye, he leaned over to give me a hug by the car door. It felt warm and sincere.

As I drove away, I realized I felt content for now. I knew we were all going to meet together sometime soon, but knowing exactly when was less important than savoring the moment we'd just shared.

8

The Courage to Reclaim
Your Connection with
Intuitive Wisdom

Weeks later, my brother, mother, Richard, and I met at my mother's house as she'd requested. It didn't take long before I realized that we had different agendas for meeting. It appeared as though Richard and my mother were there to play defense and protect their secret, whereas my brother and I were there to find out more about our family history. Whenever I'd ask family background questions, Richard would switch the subject and become playful and humorous instead of direct.

"So, Richard, what are the family nationalities on your mother and father's sides?" I curiously asked.

"Ooh . . . I don't know–Heinz 57," he said, looking over at my brother and laughing at his own comment, as if to cue my brother into laughing with him.

Hmm, I thought, *I wonder why he's avoiding my questions?*

"Well, what were their last names?" I said, looking for a more direct clue.

He paused for a moment and looked surprised that I wasn't losing my focus. Then, he shared their surnames, which clearly identified the families as Italian and English.

I slowed down the conversation in respect of his anxiety. After about another ten minutes of surface conversation, I again asked him questions. "So, I'm curious . . . Mom said you're still married to the same woman. Do you have children? I was curious about this, because I wanted to know how many half-brothers and half-sisters I have."

He confirmed that he was still married, but didn't answer my other question. So, I became more direct.

"I'm interested in knowing my half-brothers and sisters' names and ages, as well as what cities they live in. It's important to me, not because I want to contact them—I'll respect your privacy if that's what you want. But I do want to know the names, because, if they're living in the same community as me and have children that are my children's ages, I want to be sure that I know we're all related—if you know what I mean."

He quickly dismissed my question and said, "Oh, the chance of that is probably minimal. I wouldn't worry about that if I were you."

In the past, I probably would've dismissed my feelings and needs, but it was clear to me that this was important. So I reasserted my need. "I understand. You're probably right. The chances are quite slim that one of your grandchildren would date one of my children. Ooh! And that would be one of your other grandchildren too," I said, surprised at how that felt as I put it into words. "But, I'm not willing to take the slightest chance of that happening, and that's why I want to know."

I saw my mother out of the corner of my left eye. She was squirming in her chair. Richard's eyes were moving in his head, calculating his next move. I remained silent remembering the rule that I teach in my sales classes: Whoever speaks next loses.

Richard spoke next and shared his other children's names, their ages, and where they lived. I was glad I'd asked, as many of them lived in my community.

After that, I still had many more questions, but I could tell that being in the presence of the truth had saturated everyone else. Richard turned to my brother on the couch at this point and began joking around with him. I sat quietly in my observation mode, as I usually did as a kid . . . listening, watching, sensing, and feeling. The conversation was all together lacking a heartfelt connection.

It was obvious that Richard was not yet willing or capable of having a direct and detailed conversation. So, I decided to dialogue intuitively with my mother and Richard through the process I was beginning to teach in my seminars.

The first question I asked my intuition was: *Why were they attracted to one another?* As I pondered it, I employed a technique called the One-Minute Meditation. In preparation, I took several deep breaths that helped me breathe in peace and exhale anxiety. When I could feel that I was calm, I began the process of the meditation, which I refer to as the Six-Point Check.

I did the first three points of the Six-Point Check. I noticed what was going on externally by asking three questions: What am I hearing? What am I seeing? And, What am I sensing?

As I observed the people in the room, I was drawn to my mother's nonverbal language. She was sitting to my left with her legs folded, looking very proper. She was more feminine looking than I'd ever noticed before, yet stiffer. Not as flamboyant in her mannerisms as she usually appeared. It made me wonder which version of her was real. Or was neither version her authentic self?

I next turned to watch Richard and I noticed something new about him also. He looked distinguished and commanded the conversation. This was different than our first meeting, where he seemed nervous and almost powerless.

Then, I was ready to check in with myself. I did the second three points of the Six-Point Check, asking the same three questions while I focused within: What am I hearing? What am I seeing? What am I sensing?

Out of nowhere, it dawned on me that my mom was attracted to the presence of Richard's power. In the presence of his power, she could let her lady out.

Suddenly, the laughter in the room switched my attention to seeing and hearing my brother and Richard in a fencing match to be the center of attention. One witty comment cut right into the next, as they sparred back and forth demonstrating their similarities. I couldn't believe this was their first meeting. Their gestures were harmoniously orchestrated. Their humor was equally matched. Even their physical features were similar. I could see a strong resemblance. Seeing him seated side-by-side with Richard, I now knew what my brother would look like when he was 25 years older.

I turned to see my mother's reaction. She looked like a proud queen admiring her king and her prince. *Hmm,* I thought. *Isn't that interesting? No wonder my mother has always basked in my brother's presence.*

Now, I understood so much. My brother was my mother's delight because he exuded Richard's presence. Charming, entertaining, and a reminder of all the qualities she loved in Richard. That's also why Richard had looked and sounded familiar when I first heard him on the phone and then met him. On the other hand, I was the thorn who pierced the shell of Mom's denial just enough for her to feel the pain of her own lost identity and secrets.

Although I was disappointed not to learn more information at the meeting, I was mainly satisfied, as I'd received what I needed most. My eyes confirmed who my birth father was. I saw similar characteristics in us, both physically and in our personalities. My energy matched his in many ways: strong, self-assured, focused, and businesslike. Knowing that I was part Italian and part English explained my personality–passionate, yet appropriate. Most of all, I was satisfied to know my hunches were correct and I could trust my perceptions.

On my way home, I reflected on the evening. I felt somewhat the same as I do after a decent meal. Although I got to have the meat and potatoes, where was the dessert? What was missing wasn't more information; it was the caring and connected hearts. It suddenly occurred to me that we didn't leave with any next step in mind. *Hmm . . . that's interesting,* I thought.

As weeks passed, I could sense that my mother was growing anxious about the exposure of "her secret." Her old patterns of denial started to set in once again. Thus, she began attempting to control my thinking and create a mental fog for the both of us. "You know, we still don't know for sure that Richard's your father," she said on the phone three weeks after we all met.

"What do you mean, Mother?"

"Well, I said it was possible, but the more I think about it the more I think it wasn't probable."

I felt a bit annoyed with this comment, yet I fully understood what was going on. She was simply slipping back into denial due to her fear and shame. I stopped and paused for a moment, and asked my intuition: *What would be the most loving thing to say or do right now?*

"The truth in love," was my answer.

After a deep breath, I said, "Mom, it's pretty clear. What more evidence do we need? The blood types prove that Dad cannot be my biological father, and certainly my physical similarities with Richard confirm that he's my father."

"Oh, I don't know about that," she rationalized. "My grandmother had light hair like you and your brother is dark like me."

Now, I began to feel compassionate. Behind her words, I could sense her fear. "Mom, it has to be difficult for you after all of these years. I understand. I simply want to know the truth so that I can feel peace of mind."

That quieted her for the moment, but I sensed my words were only a Band-Aid covering her wound. For weeks and weeks, I was again badgered by her numerous calls attempting to convince me of the old reality.

"You know, we still don't know for sure. Chances are

he's not your birth father," she would repeat more often as time went by.

I could feel the fog of confusion settling in again. As Mom was slipping back into wishful thinking, I was tempted to do the same. Believing the old lie was less painful than going through this conflict with Mom. Her late-night phone calls grew progressively more frequent. It was as if she was trying to beat reality out of me verbally. She tried her old tactics, such as switching the focus on me, blaming me for the dilemma we were in, and then withdrawing and talking behind my back to other family members.

Then she used the tactic that cut me the deepest. She created a triangle with my brother and us: aligning with him, getting him to sympathize with her pain, and then pitting him against me as the person who'd caused the pain. I understood that my brother felt responsible for protecting my mother, being that he was the man of the house. Nonetheless, I was feeling isolated again, attacked by the two of them. Soon, he was calling me at night, too, to announce his disapproval of my need to live in the truth.

Or was it his way of keeping himself from his own truth? I wondered.

9

The Courage to Receive Truth and Speak It in "Love"

As the truth about my birth father was unraveling, so was my marital life. What gave me the most peace in the midst of the chaos was the personal relationship with God that I was beginning to develop. My husband Gary became curious about my new passion for my church and fellowship group, so he decided to check out what was going on for himself.

One night, we went to a couple's event at church. I had hoped that going to church together would make a difference. But after the event, I felt sad. The distance between us hadn't closed even though we'd shared the evening together. We got in the car and were ready to leave. He remembered that we forgot the knife we brought with the cake I'd made for the evening event.

"I'll run in and get it," he offered.

There I sat, alone in the car. Then, in the grass off to the left of the church, a cross suddenly appeared. It had always been there, I'd just never noticed. It was huge. Once it caught my complete attention, I heard a voice in my head say, "I died just for you and your sins." A flush came over my body, as I felt an incredible presence within. Yet, somehow that wasn't enough. I wanted proof.

"Save my marriage," I pleaded.

It was silent and my sadness reappeared. Then the words "Adam and Eve" came into my mind. I could see the story I'd read in the Bible as though it was happening before me. Adam and Eve were naked and hiding in the bushes from God due to their shame.

The voice reappeared,

"You are hiding from Me and each other because of your shame. You don't need to do that any longer. You are forgiven."

Energy flowed all the way through me from my head to my toes. *Wow!* I thought, *That's it. It's all about forgiveness.*

This wasn't the first time I recognized the cross. After all, I was raised Catholic. It was, however, the first time I saw it in such a personal way. This time, I recognized my need for its purpose. The cross was a reminder that I was forgiven for my pride when I made independent choices without God.

As I was noticing all of this, a vision came to me. I remembered how I got involved with Gary before my divorce from Steve was final. Sadness and shame came over me as I recalled how weak and lonely I was at that time. I felt sadness for having needed someone or something outside of myself to soothe me. I felt shame that I hadn't honored myself or my first husband enough to wait until things were completed, one way or the other, with us.

And, then, the weirdest thing happened . . . in virtually the same breath that I felt sadness and shame, I felt joy and love. I knew Jesus died for me. I was forgiven.

As I waited for my husband to return to the car, I felt a warm feeling throughout my body. Although I still didn't know what the future would bring, I did know this: I was connected and that was enough.

Unfortunately, as it is for most of us, the day-to-day stresses and distractions of life took my attention away from my euphoric experience before too long. In my case, distractions included juggling a marriage that was becoming estranged, raising two daughters, managing a growing business, and dealing with a bizarre set of circumstances regarding my birth father. Soon the feeling of peace and fulfillment was replaced by worry and anxiety.

I increased the amount of time I spent in quiet meditation. This was the only way I knew that could help me to keep my connection within while my mother was trying so hard to deny all the progress we'd made in discovering the truth about my birth father. It was exceedingly difficult to cope with the guilt my mother was placing on me when she would call late at night and say things like: "How could you do this to me!"

I knew that my past pattern under stress would be to ignore my anxiety and speed things up. That was my addiction: to deceive and betray myself by disconnecting within. Frankly, this disconnection often felt like a benefit, as it helped keep me from experiencing my own pain. Unfortunately, it also kept me from knowing what I needed to do to feel peace and self-love on an ongoing basis. I was beginning to understand that the only way to the wisdom was through the pain. Thus, I was determined to face it.

The greatest pain I was feeling at the time was fear. Diving into my fear was difficult and took courage. I knew I could no longer just put a toe in the pool of fear I was retaining. I had to take a deep breath and dive into it completely. But I feared feeling my fear. My biggest concern was what would happen if I fully embraced my fear? Would it overtake me? Finally, I surrendered to my fear and completely allowed myself to feel.

Once I allowed myself to experience the fear, I realized that the voice of fear was like a mouse speaking through a megaphone. Until I faced the mouse, I'd imagined it was a roaring lion. This awareness restored my sense of perspective.

Embracing my fear, I now asked, "What do I need to do to stay in the truth?" The answer became evident. The only way to stop the madness in my family was to get DNA testing done so that we could look at reality face on without doubt. Once I embraced that solution, I felt complete peace and self-love.

My plan didn't have the same effect initially on my mother and Richard. I guess, deep down, I'd intuitively known they wouldn't be happy with my suggestion to get DNA testing. But I was determined to stop my part in the dance, claim myself, and live in truth and peace. Going through the process of claiming my needs and speaking my truth was a bit uncomfortable. However, it helped me realize how I'd often chosen to adopt the anxiety and shame of others instead of allowing them to face their own feelings.

My suggestion to get DNA testing triggered their greatest fears. For my birth father, it was the fear that I would go to his wife with the information. He'd kept his relationship with my mother a secret from his family. After the Catholic Church told him and Mom that they would not marry them, he and his wife reconciled. My mother's biggest fear was that her mother might find out, as would her aunt, who was the President of Mount Mary College, the local Catholic college in Milwaukee. If they knew, they might disown her.

I assured them that telling the secret to his family and my relatives was never my intention. No matter what I said, however, my mother and Richard still refused to give up their control to the truth of DNA testing. There was nothing more I could do at that point except surrender, trust, and allow. It wasn't my decision to make alone.

Interestingly enough, about a month later, my mother and Richard underwent a mutual change of heart. My mother, brother, birth father, and I agreed to go get DNA testing. They'd seen that their coercing wasn't ever going to make my curiosity and conviction about my parentage disappear, so they decided to accommodate me.

After the test, we had to wait a few weeks for the results. Waiting again was hard. But I was learning how to get on with my life even as I stepped into the unknown, surrendered, asked, trusted, and allowed. Every morning I considered what I needed to do to nurture myself so that I could be at peace during this time.

Finally, the truth appeared in the mail. Richard was my birth father. My brother's DNA test confirmed that fact for him as well. I was relieved–after all, I wasn't imagining any of this! At last, I felt whole.

It didn't take long before my mother called that day. She'd also received the results in the mail. "Hi, it's Mom. Did you get your mail today?" she asked with a quiver in her voice.

"Yes, I did, Mother. The DNA results came today," I replied, knowing what question she was really asking.

She burst into tears, with a deep cry, and said, "I am so very sorry."

It was silent for a while. I didn't know what to say, so I just experienced the moment. Then she broke the silence and asked, "Can I come over and see you right now?"

I wasn't sure why she wanted to come over, but I knew we were supposed to be together. It didn't take long before we were seated at my kitchen table. I sat at the head of the table and she sat to my right. She looked deeply sorrowful. Surprisingly, the more she talked and rationalized her past behavior, the more I could feel rage flowing in my body. I didn't judge or resist the feeling. She pleaded with me to understand why she'd kept it a secret all those years.

I grew so increasingly angry that I'd been forced to live with such a crazy-making secret for so long, that I was speechless as I listened and observed her. I didn't know what to do or say.

Then, I took a couple of deep breaths. What was different in me now was that I was learning how to give my anger and pain over to God in big situations like this one. I asked God, *"What am I to learn from this?"*

As I waited, in complete anticipation, I heard the following message:

"You have both been through a great ordeal. There are many lessons for you both to learn from this situation. This would be a good time to spend time apart–for a while–so that you can both feel your own pain and learn your own lessons. One of the lessons you'll both learn is about forgiveness and love. You must forgive yourself and your mother, for you are both sinners. No sin is greater than another sin. Then, you must learn to love yourself. Only then can you live a life of peace and true love."

Upon hearing these words, I took a deep breath and felt renewed. I shared this loving truth that I just heard with my mother. I told my mother that I forgave her and myself for any pain we'd caused each other as a result of our situation. I told her that I loved her, and that I thought it would be best if we took a break from our relationship for a while. This would give us both a chance to heal and feel our own pain. She agreed . . . and so we did.

For six months after the DNA truth came out, my mother and I had little contact. We spoke once every three or four weeks just to check in with each other, but never discussed our relationship or the birth father issue. This was a boundary that we agreed on for that period of time. This was a wise decision, because my emotions vacillated from compassion to pity, to sadness, to rage. I can only imagine how her process may have been similar. Being together would have made the grieving process feel like taking a roller coaster ride.

Part of my grieving process also included my birth father. Although I was grateful that I was able to meet him and that he'd cooperated with the DNA testing, I was uncomfortable with his decision to keep my brother and me a secret. He offered to "stay in touch," but only if we did so without letting his wife or children know of our existence. I wondered, *Is this the kind of offer that he made my mother?* Living in deception was not appealing to me. For me, it would be far too great of a sacrifice of my dignity.

I remember the morning that my birth father and I last saw each other. My brother and Richard had talked a few times on the phone since the DNA testing, and then arranged for the three of us to go out for breakfast together at Denny's about a month later. When we all met, they joked about how my brother had pretended that he was a telemarketer when he called, in order to get past Richard's wife who'd answered the phone. A pit grew in my stomach as I heard about this act of deception. I couldn't help but feel sorry for his wife, living in the shadow of such a lie. When breakfast ended, after lots of talk regarding financial safety and worldwide events, he offered for us all to get together again.

"Well, I'm not sure where to go from here," he said. "You know you can call me at any time if you need me. I ask though that you be discrete when you call. I'm sure you can understand how upsetting this would be to my wife if she knew." He was making his boundaries on our relationship very clear.

"I hear your boundary," I said. "You've made it very clear that you don't want your wife or family to know about us." I was clarifying that I heard his request correctly. He nodded his head, happy that I heard him.

Then, I continued, this time to share my needs and feelings with him. "Although I can honor your request, I can't see the possibility for a healthy relationship under those terms. If someday you choose to tell your family, I'd be open to exploring what kind of relationship we could develop. Until then, it wouldn't feel right to me."

Although I could see by the look on his face that he

was a bit taken back by my response, I was more aware of how awesome it felt to claim my own truth and speak it in "love." It gave me a free and powerful feeling inside. I could feel loving energy flowing through my body. In my mind's eye I saw the shape of an "L," as I pictured the connection happening within me. It was as though the energy was flowing into the top of my head from way up in the sky, through my heart, and out to my birth father.

Then Richard spoke in a flippant manner, "Okay, if that's the way you need it to be, that's fine."

I could sense that something had just shifted in my emotional energy field. *What is it?* I wondered. *Oohh . . . yuck! It feels like I was just made into the one who is responsible for this relationship ending.* I knew that I didn't like the way that felt, so I went within and asked my intuitive guidance, *What do I need to do or say here in "love"?*

Once I knew what I was to say, I took a deep breath and looked him square in the eyes. I paused for a moment and reiterated in a gentle voice what I'd said a moment before. I did this with the intention of putting the responsibility back in his lap in a loving way. "I will honor your request to keep this a secret from your family. If someday you choose to tell your family about my brother and me, I would be open to exploring what kind of relationship we could develop."

Richard acknowledged what I said by nodding his head. He then quickly stood up and grabbed the bill off of the table. We all walked to the cashier together and said good-bye rather abruptly. It was awkward, but I understood why–truth can be like that sometimes.

That was the last time I spoke with Richard. For about six months, my brother Gary tried to stay in contact with him, but was eventually disappointed with the one-sided nature of the relationship he experienced, which continued to be a secret. So, in the end, we all ended up parting ways.

Although some of the outcomes in my story are not like those in fairytales, the magical part came when I committed to living in the truth, and claimed my inner knowing and myself over my desire to bond with others. Every time I experienced the upward and inner flow of making authentic connections, I could see the "L" shape again in my mind's eye. It was happening more often. I was deceiving and betraying myself less, and honoring and loving myself, as well as others, more.

Contemplating my new way of being one day, a voice appeared in my head,

"You are learning to live in the 'L,' with the courage to receive and speak the truth 'in love.'"

My life was growing more content even though everything around me seemed to be falling apart. This included my marriage, which had been on rocky ground for a few years. Within a few months after my birth father and I parted company, my second marriage ended. My husband had a difficult time withstanding the turmoil and all the changes I was undergoing, so he filed for divorce. I felt sad about his decision, but somehow understood that I no longer was the same person with whom he fell in love. Interestingly, this time I wasn't as scared to be alone as I was the first time I got divorced. In fact, part of me was excited about the new adventure ahead.

Well, adventure it was . . . starting the day after my husband moved out! It began with me going to buy a dresser to replace the one he took from our bedroom set. As the young gentleman from the furniture store was helping me jimmy it into the back of my car, I suddenly felt something crash onto the top of my head. I wasn't sure what hit me, as I doubled over and fell to the ground. Minutes later, I regained consciousness, only to find out that he'd mistakenly closed the hatchback trunk on my head! For weeks, I suffered from a concussion and had to endure bed rest as I recovered.

With a severe concussion, I no longer could rely on the skills that normally helped me perform. Not only was my energy taken away, so were my abilities to focus and articulate myself. If you've ever had a concussion, you know what I mean. I couldn't even recall words to explain techniques I'd been teaching for years, let alone put my thoughts into words. This is a huge problem for someone who relies on these skills to make her living as a trainer, coach, and seminar speaker!

I must admit that although I was looking forward to an adventure, I wasn't quite ready for this one! It was scary, because I was worrying, *How long will this concussion last? Will I ever fully recover? Will the furniture store remunerate me for my loss of earnings?* As I searched to find the deeper meaning of these questions, I realized I was facing the fear of *Am I enough? Will life support me enough? Will I have enough?* As I became more aware of my fear, I could embrace and then release it.

There was so much of me to be discovered, so much I didn't know. I had not taken the time to truly claim who I was authentically up until this point. So much of my life was a lie. My choices until then had focused more on pleasing and accommodating others, and on performing well, rather than on manifesting my heart's desire.

The adventure in front of me was going to be a time of recovery from my head injuries: the one that took place at the furniture store and the one that took place in my childhood. Because my memory recall was poor, I was forced to be extremely present with whatever experience the moment would bring.

As it turned out, the recovery time took longer than I expected. It was about a month before I could work and about six months before I felt completely back to normal. During the healing period, I learned to let go of self-reliance and ask for support. I also learned to trust that I was enough with or without the gifts I usually relied on. As a result of the head injury, I had to learn how to rely less on my intellect and more on my sensing ability.

In the past, I'd gone to God with the most aching question in my heart, *"Who is my birth father?"* Although He was faithful in answering me, now I needed help with my insecurity in the moment. I asked: *"Who will love me and take care of me?"* The head injury was the catalyst for me to depend more on God to support my family and me. Could I learn to rely on Him rather than myself (or a man) for all of my needs? Could I give my inner most feelings to Him? This was going to be the next great lesson in my life.

It wasn't until almost a year later that a significant test was put before me that would teach me to claim my authentic self, listen to my intuition, and begin to learn to trust in God to take care of me.

A difficult situation showed up at work. I had done business with the specific client it involved a year previously and could still remember how difficult the training sessions were because of the oppressed culture at the company. The employees were full of a lot of fear because change happened too rapidly there, with little regard for the emotions of the people involved.

It was a government agency in Iowa, where many employees originally took their jobs for security. However, the new leadership was running the corporate culture with a bottom-line mentality. There was no such thing as a secure job any longer.

"We have a program that we want you to handle for us immediately. It's called a Competency Program and management wants to get it done before the end of the year," the Human Resources Director told me in early October. He continued, "I must warn you, the company is very budget conscious."

I told the Director that I needed to understand more about the program and the parameters before I would accept the job. As far as the dates, I shared with him that it was unlikely that I would be able to complete the project in the timeline they were hoping for, since I was booked solid until the end of the year. I asked for a list of the competencies and the numbers of employees involved, so I could put a proposal together for him and look at what might be possible.

As soon as we hung up the phone, I got a queasy sensation in the pit of my stomach. *Hmm . . . I wonder what that feeling is about?* I inquired within–and this time I chose to pay attention to the wisdom of my anxiety.

It didn't take long before I knew what the sensation was about. I remembered how draining the last project had been with this agency. I knew what they were asking me to do still wasn't addressing their root cause. It was a Band-Aid approach to a problem that required deep surgery. Motivating the employees to "buy-in" to these required competencies was going to take a tremendous amount of energy. Furthermore, it sounded like they didn't have the budget that would be needed to do the job right. Having that much information right at the "tip of the iceberg", made me pause. I wondered, *What do I need to do or say in this situation for the Highest Good of All?*

When I next spoke with my contact, the Human Resources Director, he confirmed their budget constraints. He also shared additional parameters to the program. Not only did they want me to cut my fee by 25 percent, they wanted to add 160 people to the program, and have me sign over the copyrights to them. They also wanted me to sign an agreement that stated they could let me go at any time, for any reason, with a ten-day notice.

I couldn't believe it! Was this how they treated their employees: ask for more, but give them less? I would have had to be pretty hard up to accept those terms. So I declined the project, encouraged them to call me in the future if they had other needs, and thanked them for considering me once again.

My contact called me a few days later and said his boss wanted to talk to me about the program over lunch. Although at this point I felt exhausted and uninterested in taking on the client, I wanted to remain open to what he might have to say. Little did I know that his intention was to convince me that my boundaries were unacceptable to him.

When I met with him at lunch, I empathized with his needs. But when I shared that I wasn't willing or able to meet them, he became very demeaning. At that point, he grabbed his silverware to demonstrate his experience of the distance in our negotiation. He was quite blatant about his opinion that the inability to come to terms was my fault.

In a very condescending manner, he went on to say, "This is what it's like working with you," as he picked up his fork and laid it down on the table. "This is what you want, and it's more than any other consultant I've ever worked with," he continued.

Then he picked up his knife from the table. "This is what I need to make this program work." He placed the knife six inches from the fork. Then he pulled out the spoon. "And this," he said, "is what you say you'll give." He placed the spoon only a half of an inch away from the fork showing that, from his perception, I didn't budge much from my original parameters. Then, he looked up at me with disgust, continuing, "And you say you're compromising?"

I could tell he expected his drama to create a sense of

insecurity and shame inside of me. I wondered if he thought that the demonstration would actually make me want to take on the project. Even more so, I wondered, *Who taught him that intimidation tactic?* I checked in with myself and realized that I felt self-assured and connected.

I smiled at him and said, "Yes, that's pretty accurate . . . except for a little twist to how I see it." Then, I shared my experience with him using the same silverware.

"You're right, this is where my expectations are. And you're right, we are this far apart. And you're right, I'm not willing to compromise what I deserve or what I know works. As I see it . . . there will be a problem if you don't get exactly what you want." I looked at him deeply in his eyes, as I continued, "You see, I'm at the point in my career where I'll only take a job if I know it will work. It's also important to me that my work be fun. This type of interaction is not what I am looking for in a business relationship."

That afternoon, I declined the job. I knew it was the right decision for me, because I felt full of delight and peace inside. Speaking my truth and maintaining my dignity sure felt good. Even though the outcome didn't look successful, the process itself was exactly what I needed to reclaim my authentic self and my intuitive wisdom.

On the drive home, I couldn't help but wonder, *What was really going on with him? Why was he so attached to convincing me to take the job?"*

Two days later, I found out from another company contact that the boss was shocked I didn't take the money. He couldn't believe I would just pass up $35,000 for a project at the drop of a hat. Interestingly, I learned he'd been in a consulting business like mine several years ago. The rumor was that he'd had to close his doors because he couldn't make a living supporting his family. I wondered if, perhaps, he wasn't charging enough. In any case, I knew that our little exercise, at some level, was enlightening for both of us.

Although I didn't know exactly what the future would be in detail or what the timing of things would be as circumstances in my life unfolded, I was learning to trust in myself and in my intuition. I now believed that I could be mindful in choosing the situations I wanted to be in and how I wanted to behave in them in each moment. All I needed to do was check-in within. Decisions were right for me when I felt passionate and at peace. The question I used now that gave me the most clarity was: What is real and true here?

Waiting for the answer to this question before I acted or spoke made me feel confident in my subsequent choices. Asking and then meditating ensured I was listening to my heart and to Spirit's calling instead of my ego's need. There were two additional steps that kept me on track. First, I would check in regarding big decisions with a group of people who were in my accountability group. Secondly, I spent time with the Living Word, the Bible. Because I was measuring the decisions I was making against values that were written on my heart, I could more easily trust them, even if the outcomes of those decisions didn't turn out exactly as I wanted or thought they would.

Asking for clarity and answers always brought truth, but not necessarily right away. At times that wasn't a problem. At other times, it was a concern, because I, like most people, felt I needed to have an answer immediately at times. An example is a work situation when performance was needed in the moment. For me, this was most true when I was doing my weekly radio show "Performance Solutions" and a listener called in, or when I was doing coaching and had to know what to do or say on the spot.

When I needed an answer immediately, I did the same One-Minute Meditation I'd used months earlier when I was observing my family dynamics. In fact, this was a technique that I unconsciously did for years without giving it a name. It wasn't until several clients had asked me how I could be so intuitive that I named the steps I took while I was opening up to receive truth. Once I articulated the process, I began to use it more and teach it in sessions as well.

Even with this technique, however, there are limitations, for, as humans, we're limited. The more I saw my new methods helping leaders and employees, the more I felt that I was living on purpose. Yet, I continued to be curious . . . Could we ever completely trust in our perceptions and ourselves? What else was needed for us to be able to handle the unexpected twists and turns in life with more ease and grace?

As I pondered what was missing from the equation, I could see and sense that the heart and soul were often absent in relationships and at work. I wondered, *What would happen if we began to talk about topics like heart and soul under circumstances where it would often be considered inappropriate?* Were these words too "soft and fuzzy" for business settings, or did we only think so because the legal separation of Church and State made us believe we couldn't talk about spirituality at all? Perhaps we had thrown the baby out with the bath water and omitted all the good that came from bringing our heart and Spirit to relationships and work.

Upon honest assessment, wouldn't you say that too many of us spend most of our time focused on issues of deprivation, such as: Will I have enough money at retirement? Will my marriage be good enough to meet my needs? Will I get enough love? Will I have a good enough job? Will I have enough time? Will I have a purpose someday that will fulfill me enough? Will my kids turn out good enough? Can I trust myself enough?

Intuitively, I was aware that neither self-knowledge nor connecting with our intuition and gut feeling could solve the problem of deprivation thinking. It would take something bigger than us to solve this problem. I also knew I might be hitting on a sensitive nerve where people would have very strong opinions if I brought Spirit into the workplace.

My Christian friends advised me to "be bold for Christ" in my career. But that didn't seem to be the answer in and of itself. Yes, I am a follower of Christ, but I didn't want to talk about theology or salvation. I was concerned with the spiritual need to relinquish control in the face of uncertainty and adversity. Even many longtime believers that I know struggle with the tendency to control.

So, then what was the answer? My non-religious friends told me that any mention of God in my work might limit my audience, especially if I intended to reach out to the general public and go into the workplace. Not only would it be "inappropriate," they warned me, it would be "offensive" to many.

I wrestled to understand these conflicting points of view and to find my truth. Could it be that most people have developed a spiritual ego of sorts, and are so busy to prove they have all the right answers that they're closed off from each other and, worse yet, from the Spirit within? Or have some people just become so disgusted with religious institutions that they've given up on their whole spiritual lives all together?

In either case, when I peeled back all the differences between various religions and theologies, one thing remained in common: core values and beliefs like "In God we trust," "Love one another as your self," and "Forgive one another." Although the followers of different religions and philosophies may phrase these ideas differently, the message is the same: Trust and love!

One day, I contemplated the coins I had in my wallet. I wondered, *Do they still have "In God We Trust" on them?* It had been so long since I stopped and looked at one closely that I didn't know for sure, so I opened my wallet to check. It was still there. How often this phrase passes through our hands, yet we so rarely stop pursuing our busyness to think about what it really means.

I thought about my clients and all the situations in the workplace that are potential catalysts to trigger those feelings hidden deep within to erupt. What would be their choice in such situations? Would they continue to fight or flee, or would we together develop another, "third door" option?

I knew my mission was to bring heart and spirit back into our moment-to-moment lives, but I didn't yet know how it would be possible. If for no one else, I was determined to find a way for myself to have this experience in my own work and relationships. I knew this was my purpose, because my passion to do so now outweighed fear of any outcome it might produce.

The adventure in front of me felt exciting. I no longer was only the teacher, I was also the student. It was comforting to know that I was learning to die to self-reliance and self-will by replacing my timeworn belief "If it's meant to be, it's up to me" with "How might I do God's will?"

As I looked back at my life, I thought about how often I took control by steering my course only to find I had fallen into some deep, dark pit. I knew I wasn't alone in this, as I remembered a Buddhist story of enlightenment that my friend Jan had shared with me taken from *The Tibetan Book of Living and Dying* by Sogyal Rinpoche. It reveals the journey we all take as we slowly learn how to make better decisions in our life. The story reveals four stages of development. Initially, we do not want to take responsibility for our choices, and tend to claim that the consequences are not our fault. Then, in stage two, although we continue to make the same choices, and we still do not take responsibility, at some level we know these choices are not good for us.

The third stage marks the time of recognition. We know our patterns and tendencies, and although we may sometimes make choices that are not best for us, we take responsibility and quickly make necessary changes. At our final stage of development and awareness, we do not make decisions until we are clear about the possibilities before us, which may include radically different choices.

In reading the story, I realized how important it is to give ourselves grace along the way, as we are all here to learn how to do this in our everyday moments.

We're ready for the next Secret to "I AM" when we can experience the pitfalls in our paths as blessings. They are given to us, in love, to help create the shift from old patterns of self-reliance and self-protection to awareness of our need for a power greater than ourselves to show us the way.

The Fourth Secret:

*Embrace a Love in Something
Bigger than Yourself*

It's not what you do,
It's how you do it.
So, do it with all the
Love you have within.

ASK:
*"How might I be a vessel of love
in this situation?"*

10

The Courage to Be Grateful for the Lessons of Love

Much of my journey to this point had been about learning to trust my inner wisdom and myself. I was grateful for having healed my old wound of self-doubt and my reactive pattern of fear, judgment, and control, which led me either to flee in the face of difficulty or to fight to make it happen my way! Already, I was checking within more regularly for guidance. Yet, I was still left unsatisfied at times–in fact, too often.

My life as a single mom lasted seven years and was fairly adventurous. During that time, I grew my consulting business and my radio show, and I grew up a lot too! My children, Lisa and Alex, grew in positive ways as well, in spite of the fact that my two divorces could easily have had a negative impact on them. I feared that possibility. In reality, my circumstances ultimately weren't as important to their development as being raised in a home that was filled with truth, love, a philosophy of being open, and the trust that "all things are possible through the power of God."

In addition to my work and kids, life offered me many opportunities to enjoy my time alone or with friends, family, and dating when my children would go away every other weekend. In this period of my life, I was learning what I really wanted out of life and in a relationship with a man.

About six years after my divorce, my acquaintance Kathy called to see if I could train her new "employee at the front desk" in customer service and sales at a single's dating service she'd just bought. Kathy and I had known each other well over 20 years earlier when we'd both worked at the Barbizon School of Modeling. When she found out that I had divorced, she suggested that I take out a membership to meet the available men in town through her service.

"I don't think so, Kathy. I believe in meeting a guy naturally," I told her emphatically. "Plus, the last thing I want to have happen is for one of my clients to see me in one of your profile books. That would be very uncomfortable."

"Well, here's what we can do," she said. "We can place you in a confidential file. I know you and understand what you are looking for in a relationship. If a qualified gentleman comes in, you'll be the first to know. You can check out his profile first, and decide about him, without him ever knowing."

"Really? Do you actually have guys in your service that you think I might be interested in dating?"

"You'd be surprised," she said, reassuring me that it would be a positive experience.

So I did–I signed up! And she was right . . . it was one of the best experiences I ever had. The best part was being able to meet all different kinds of people, some who looked so compatible with me on paper, but often ended up being nothing like that at all! Then there were the others who, if not for Kathy, I would never have noticed. They often ended up being the men with whom I had the most fun. I dated short guys, tall guys, thin guys, chubby guys, guys that were entrepreneurs, guys that were doctors, guys that were college educated, and some that weren't. I dated guys to whom I was physically attracted but with whom I couldn't hold a conversation, and others whom I found so interesting but with whom I could never feel the chemistry. Finally, after being a member in the dating service for almost a year, only two weeks before my contract was due to expire, I received a voice mail from Kathy at the dating service.

"Hey Sue, a guy just signed up today and I really

think he's the guy you've been waiting to meet. He's expressed wanting a lot of the same things you've expressed. He's a person who is family-oriented, fun, interested in becoming friends first, attractive, and Christian. He says he's a financial investor. Give me a call, let's talk about it."

The next day, I called Kathy and went in to see the man's profile and video. Immediately, I was attracted to the way he presented himself as real and down to earth. Just listening to his video and seeing him made me feel a connection that I had not felt with a man since my divorce.

I thanked Kathy for the lead and let her know I was interested. So she gave Tom, the guy in the profile, a call to come on in and see my video and profile as well. A few days later, I received a call from him on a Friday night at about six o'clock. We chatted on the phone for 20 minutes and had a pretty easy connection on the phone. I distinctly remember feeling that the conversation was more real than some of the others were at the start, which was one of the biggest qualities I was looking for in a person.

We did exactly what both of us said we wanted to do—we took it slowly and spent time getting to know each other. For the next two weeks, we talked on the phone every other night before we actually met. Besides wanting to take it slow, he also admitted suffering recently from a terrible back injury.

"How'd that happen?" I inquired, wondering if he did it working.

"I don't know—it came out of nowhere."

"Well, did you do anything unusually physical?"

"No . . . but it did start hurting on the plane on the way back from a trip I recently took."

"Where is the pain in your back?"

"It's in my lower lumbar area."

"Hmm . . . that's interesting. You know, I own a mind-body-spirit book that says the lower back is related to money issues. Do you have money issues of any kind?"

"Let's put it this way: money has been a stress lately. There's been a lot of change around it for me."

I wondered why he was being so ambiguous around the subject of money. Although I didn't inquire more directly, I certainly made a note of that conversation and asked my intuition to pay attention.

Suddenly, he interrupted my deep curiosity, "We've been chatting on the phone for almost two weeks now. I'm wondering, are you ready to meet in person yet? I was kind of waiting to see if my back would feel better, but I'm not convinced that's going to happen soon," he explained.

"Yes, I am ready to meet."

"Great. How does Friday work?"

"I'd like that, but I won't be home from a training session until about six o'clock."

"Then I'll call you at 6:30 and we can see what we feel up to at the time."

"Perfect, I'm looking forward to meeting you in person."

So, Friday night came and went and there was no call from Tom. Although I was disappointed that he didn't call, it didn't feel like he stood me up. It felt like something else, but I couldn't put my finger on it . . . at least, not until Sunday at church. There I was, in a pew with two friends of mine, singing the day's hymns. It wasn't until I was completely relaxed and into the moment that I heard a still, small voice inside say, "He's in the hospital with his back. He doesn't have your number."

As usual, I became curious. *Hmm . . . isn't that interesting? What am I to do?*

"Call him and leave your number on his voice mail," I heard.

So I did. I called as soon as I got home and left a

message on his voice mail saying, "Hi, Tom. I was at church this morning and had the oddest feeling that you're in the hospital and don't have my number with you. I'm leaving it on your voice mail just in case."

Sure enough, a half-hour later my caller ID showed Waukesha Memorial Hospital on it.

"Hi. Guess where I am," he said, as he quickly interrupted my hello.

"Tom . . . is that you?"

"Yes. How did you know I was in the hospital? I was worried you'd think I stood you up. I didn't have your number."

"Are you okay?"

"Now I am. But I passed out on Friday after a cortisone shot and they rushed me to the hospital. I had surgery just hours later."

"Oh, you're kidding. Can I come see you and bring you a balloon or a candy bar to cheer you up?"

"Now it's my turn . . . are you kidding?" He asked playfully.

"No, not at all. You obviously don't know me yet, or you wouldn't be asking that question," I said, enjoying our little sparring game.

"But I haven't showered for two days."

"Really, do you smell a lot or just look bad?"

"I think a little bit of both."

"Hmm . . . well, if it's only a little bit, I think I can handle it. How about if I come on up in a few hours?"

"Okay, but I warned you."

I laughed as we hung up the phone. Again, I was happy that I could trust in my intuition. *I was right!* I proudly thought.

Well, that marked the beginning of our romance and my lessons in love. Upon entering the hospital room two hours later, my eyes were drawn to an IV hooked up to Tom's arm. Being that I don't like hospitals, I was already getting a bit queasy. Then I heard his voice . . .

"Wow, you're beautiful."

I smiled as I saw his face light up. Receiving his genuine compliment while still feeling quite playful, I looked at his IV once again and said, "Yeah, and you're on drugs."

We laughed, as our eyes met and stayed connected for the first time.

After days of visiting and weeks of his recovery, Tom and I began to date regularly. There was one time in particular, about four months afterwards, that I felt a sense of knowing that our lives had a deep purpose together. It was the day that we decided to volunteer our time and talents to serve a local church administration that was struggling with leadership and teamwork issues.

For me, the best part was before the program even started, when Tom and I met at about 7:30 a.m. Tom was dressed in his khaki outdoor clothing and was already making our coffee with his camping gear when I met him at the campground. He was in his element. I could feel his center and his heart, and it was so attractive. We sat together on the top of a picnic table, enjoying the perfect summer day. As I was watching him pour our coffee, I could see our lives coming together for a purpose in my mind's eye. This was what I wanted so much: to serve God with a partner in life!

As I saw the vision in my mind, I felt warmth come over my body, and then he grabbed my hand. "Let's pray for the people who will be here, before they get here. Okay? Let's pray for openness and learning." Wow! The energy that flowed from the top of my head to the tip of my toes was incredible. This moment felt like the perfect connection.

It wasn't long before the participants arrived at the park, reminding us that we had a teamwork program to lead. Together, we greeted them and informed them of the day's activities and our roles. I was the training facilitator while Tom was the experiential expert. Because of his experience from the Marines, Tom was able to develop a compass course that could be used to demonstrate leadership and teamwork tendencies in the field. We'd developed it so that the staff would have to communicate and collaborate in order to find their way out of Kettle Moraine, a nearby national park. It was interesting to see how the same dynamics showed up in the park as in the church office!

The day went as I expected. The people went into their usual reactive patterns complaining that the directions weren't good enough, their team members weren't open enough, they weren't given enough time, and so on. I wasn't surprised. This is what the experience was supposed to do: bring out their natural reactive tendencies.

But Tom was devastated with all of the complaints. I had failed to warn him that it wasn't personal! Whereas I had done this for nearly 15 years and knew complaints were part of the process, he took them very personally and felt a lot of shame. Even though I tried to explain what had happened, his shame was deeper than my words could reach. He went into a major flight pattern, and disregarded any interest in doing this type of work together again in the future.

Yet, I trusted that all things would work out in perfect timing. So, I let go and began to trust and allow. I knew that if we were supposed to work together doing programs like this one, the opportunity would unfold. There was so much more about Tom and our relationship to learn about that I felt satisfied with the way things were right then.

For months, we continued to spend time just getting to know each other. After about six months, we were discussing the possibility of marriage and decided to go to Detroit to look at wedding rings together at my uncle's jewelry store. It didn't take long before we found the perfect ring to symbolize our relationship. It was an unusual ring that had two pillars of diamonds, one on each side of the center stone. We both liked it because it was a visual picture of "two pillars of strength in the Lord."

Later that weekend, when Tom and my Uncle Jon went back to get the ring, I was waiting with anticipation. When they returned, they told me that the jeweler cracked the setting from the heat and they would have to reorder a new one. Since I'd become so connected with my feelings, I began to cry from great disappointment. But, little did I know that, later that night, Tom would be waiting for just the perfect moment, from his perspective, to ask me to be his wife.

I must admit I was somewhat disappointed. The proposal didn't happen through the traditional dinner or banner sign at the ballgame like I expected. Instead, Tom waited for an uneventful moment when he felt we were really connected emotionally. Normally, I would have appreciated that . . . but what kind of story would that be for me to tell for the rest of my life? Although not glamorous, it was sincere. Tom explained all the reasons he loved me and wanted to share his life with me, including how he loved my sensitivity.

During our engagement, we continued to ask God to show us the way, including which house we were to buy or build so that we could blend our family of five children together. Our first mistake came when we both exclaimed, "This will not be an easy task!" Sure enough, that's what happened. We got exactly what we expected.

One night, shortly after we were engaged, we dropped off my daughter Alex at a church function during the week. I suggested we take a scenic route back to my condo so that we could go through a subdivision that I always liked. As we were driving, we saw a house put up for sale. It was the one I'd always admired! We didn't say much about it to each other except to share our surprise. We weren't planning on getting married for another six months, so it was one of those "unexpected moments" in life that I thought we were just acknowledging.

Then, something strange happened. That night, when I went to bed, I had a dream. I dreamed that we bought a house that had a spiral staircase and a large two-story fireplace in it. Those were the only two details I remembered from the dream other than a feeling I also vaguely remembered. I remembered being in the laundry room of the house and gazing out a window that overlooked water. I also remembered feeling sad, but I didn't know why.

The next morning, I didn't take much time to process the dream, because I'd overslept and needed to get off to work for an early morning teamwork session downtown. Usually, Tom and I would chat on the phone before work to discuss how we'd slept and what was in store for the day. But, that morning, we spoke for only a few minutes. In that short five minutes, I only shared with him that I had a weird dream and I would fill him in on the details later.

As I was busy training, Tom was busy calling our Realtor to see if he could get in the house that we'd stumbled upon the night before. He thought that would make me happy. By lunch, he had already gone inside the house that was for sale and he was quite excited. He called me on my cell phone and left a message on voicemail.

When I took my lunch break and called in for messages, I could hear his enthusiasm as he described what he saw. "Hey, Sue. You'll never believe it! I got into that house we saw the other night that was for sale. It was great! It's perfect for us. Not only does it have the master bedroom on the first floor like we wanted, it also has a great spiral staircase and beautiful two-story fireplace! From the back of the house you can see a pond."

I couldn't believe my ears! Could it be the house in my dream? I needed to find out, so I quickly called him. "I heard your message. You sounded pretty excited. Did you say it had a spiral staircase in it?"

"Yeah, right when you walk in."

"Did you happen to notice whether the house has a laundry room with a window in it that faces the water?"

"Yes, in fact it does. Why do you ask?"

"Well . . . remember I told you that I had this weird dream last night? Guess what the dream was about? I dreamed about a house that had a spiral staircase, a two-story fireplace, and a laundry room with a window in it that faced the water."

"Wow! You're kidding me!"

"No, I'm not. But there was one thing I didn't understand in the dream. I was feeling some fear and sadness when I was standing in the laundry room. It was vacant–without a washer and dryer. I'm not sure what that was about."

"Well, maybe we need to go see it and see what happens."

"That sounds like a good idea. But Tom, isn't this a lot sooner than we planned?" I asked, wondering if we were jumping the gun on buying a house.

"Well, I guess so. But let's just go with the flow and see where it takes us."

"Okay," I said, somewhat hesitant, yet open.

That night, we saw the house together and fell in love with it. It needed a lot of work, including a whole remodel of the basement. We needed to build two more bedrooms and a new bathroom in order to have enough space for our five kids, who ranged in age from 8 to 20 at the time.

We contemplated buying the house and prayed about it for over a month before we finally put in an offer. We decided that if our offer should be accepted we would move our wedding date up by three months and then sell the homes we currently lived in when the remodeling was almost finished.

We closed on our new house in the middle of August 2001. It was exciting for a few weeks, as we picked out colors and shopped together for flooring, carpeting, and other necessary things that would make this house our home. Then, at about 9:00 a.m. on the morning of September 11, 2001, my condo doorbell rang. I was getting ready for a training session at noon. Tom was at the door. He was frantic.

"What?" I said.

"Did you hear?"

"Hear what?"

"Did you hear about the towers?"

"What are you talking about?"

Tears were flowing down his cheeks. I had no idea what he was talking about. I had spent the morning in quiet time and was now getting ready for work. He rushed to my TV set and turned it on. A plane had just hit the World Trade Center towers in New York moments before he'd turned on the TV. He began crying even harder.

My first thoughts went to a former college roommate, Kris, whom I knew worked on Park Avenue in downtown Manhattan. *Is she okay?* I wondered. Kris worked for Donnelley Printing and had several clients in the towers. *Was it possible that she had called on one of them that morning?* I quickly called New York trying to reach her, but only got a busy signal. After attempting for half an hour, I finally tried her parents who lived in Wisconsin, only to receive their voice mail. I let them know of my concern, and waited, like so many other families and friends who were also in the unknown. Then, the broadcaster began to talk about Wall Street. Suddenly, another thought came to me. Now my thoughts turned to money and security.

"Tom, do you still have your money in the stock market?"

He had won the lottery less than a year before I met

him. It wasn't until almost three months into our relationship that he explained that this was why he was investing. He had gone into a gas station to buy a cup of coffee one day and decided to invest a dollar in a lottery ticket. He purchased the ticket and found out later that week that he had won several million dollars. He was an electrician at the time, so this was pretty incredible news!

Life really changed that day for Tom, and more so in the months that followed. He went from being barely able to pay his bills, to having several million dollars, to having just slightly over one million by the time the Wisconsin Lottery took their part, taxes took their part, and child support got its part. This all happened within the first year after he won the lottery. Now I was wondering if 9/11 was going to get a part of it too.

"Yes, I still have it invested with my stockbroker."

"Well, I think this incident is going to affect the market in a big way. Wall Street just got hit. I think you ought to call your stockbroker right now and discuss the facts and possibilities with him regarding this new situation."

"Oh my gosh! I never thought about that. I think you're right," he said. So he called right away, but there was nothing his broker could do.

"Everything's shut down," his broker told him.

It wasn't until about a week later that Tom was able to look at the current state of his portfolio. He had lost nearly 20 percent of his money, which now put him under a million dollars. Although this was still more than he ever thought he would earn in a lifetime as an electrician, he was devastated by the turn of events that occurred over the last few years. He had gone from collecting almost $15,000 a month in dividends, before all the cuts were taken, to now collecting no dividend at all, because it was out of the market.

Although we were both happy in the end that we

hadn't lost any friends or family in the tragic incident, our fears regarding our economic uncertainty and day-to-day safety were now the focus. This was very personal to Tom. So was the possibility of him going to war, since Tom still had a few months left in his military term. It didn't take long before he was consumed by nightmares, wondering if we would go to war and if his name would be called for active duty.

Now, I was becoming a bit concerned too. Was it possible that I finally found true love and he could actually be called off to war? This is not what I had bargained for, yet I knew that I needed to deal with my fear of loss and just stay open.

So we did that. We continued on with our plans and stayed open. One of the things we considered was the possibility of selling our homes earlier than we had originally planned. We thought and prayed about it and decided to put them on the market and see what happened. My condo sold within ten days, and we agreed to take the offer since it was for the full asking price. Little did we know that this would start a series of unexpected events. We would be put in the unknown in a profound way in order to stretch our faith and develop trust in something bigger than our selves and our plans.

The first unexpected change had to do with the closing date. Our buyer had an offer to sell her house and needed to move up the closing date by six weeks. Again, we prayed. We decided that on our end we could make changes to renovation deadlines and wedding plans. We were planning a very small wedding in our home and our pastor was available to accommodate the shift.

Shortly after this decision, life became even more stressful, and the fun turned into chaos. Contractors were missing deadlines and nothing was going as planned. Both of us began to fall into reactive patterns. We were starting to see the worst in each other. The more I pushed to make things happen, the more Tom resisted and dug in his heels, like a donkey resisting being led.

Then, only weeks before the wedding and the day before my move, we got a call from our buyer's attorney. Our buyer, who was in her 60s, had a nervous breakdown. Now they wanted to postpone the closing to see if she still wanted to move from the home that she' d had for 25 years once she was better.

What were we to do now? There were so many unknown factors. Was this a sign of trouble ahead or just an inconvenience? As we were sitting amongst boxes the night before my scheduled move, we discussed our plans. Both of us agreed that things had not been fun the last six weeks, but that we could understand due to the circumstances. We therefore decided to continue on in good faith. We dealt with what was before us, including moving me, knowing we might have to put the condo up for sale a second time if she backed out.

But things didn't let up! The week before our wedding was even more chaotic. Tom's ex-wife was making threats to call her attorney because she wanted to change the schedule. Our buyer backed out of the deal on my condo, and our renovation was not done. This meant our children didn't have their own bedrooms to move into. I felt like Adam and Eve in the garden. We had so much, yet we were pointing our fingers and blaming each other for the horrific dilemma we perceived we were in.

As we approached the final few days before the wedding, we met with our pastor for the last time in preparation. We shared with him how we weren't getting along due to all the stresses with which we had to deal. He empathized with our situation and suggested we pray about what to do. He said, "If you want me to do the wedding I will. If you feel you need more time, just let me know. I will be okay with your decision if you want to postpone it until things have settled down."

So we talked and prayed some more, and decided to carry on.

The day of our wedding was beautiful. It was December and we had decorated a Christmas tree that stretched high enough to meet the two-story ceiling in our living room, where we had our small and intimate home wedding. And believe it or not, God performed a miracle: the kids' bedrooms were finished the day before the wedding! Yet, with all the stress and busyness, I felt disconnected from my husband-to-be, who was working until the very last minute to get things done. Although grateful, I felt sad that we didn't have the time to savor all the preparations.

When the wedding night was over and we came back home from the Wisconsin Club after the dinner reception, we chatted about what part of the evening was our favorite. We both agreed it was when we took our vows. We wrote them ourselves and included that we wanted "God to remove all the blocks that kept us from loving each other completely."

Little did we know that God was going to do exactly what we asked in our vows. Although He allowed the "honeymoon stage" to last a few weeks, shortly after that we were being renovated in a BIG way!

About two and a half months after we were married, a pivotal moment happened that was a catalyst in setting the course for the next year of our marriage. We'd been having a difficult time staying open to and trusting each other as we made decisions together in regards to our blended-family. Tom was used to having his kids 50 percent of the time and being the head of his household, while I was used to having mine 80 percent of the time and being the head of my household.

Although I taught collaboration in the workplace, we were having a hard time doing that together at home. In hindsight, it's easy to see that we were both attached to believing our way was the right way. Even more so, now I can see that both of us were afraid of being controlled and losing ourselves to someone else like we had each done before.

Many nights, both of us felt frustrated with the other when we went to bed, because of a disagreement. What happened to this relationship in which I thought we had so much in common? No answers appeared other than, "It takes time to build a team." I knew this because I taught teambuilding. So we carried on.

Then, one afternoon, months into our marriage, Tom took me out to lunch. We thought this would be a great way to connect and carve out space for ourselves away from the kids. That morning, right before he came to get me at my office, my phone rang. It was a church friend who shared how another church friend's husband had admitted to using pornography and prostitutes during the last year in their marriage.

"Are you sure?" I said.

She said, "Yes. His wife found some odd charges on his credit card and confronted him. He eventually admitted it. My husband is speaking to him as we speak."

This was a couple that had been married for several years and served at church for as long as I knew them. The news hit me at the core, penetrating to my fear that I carried throughout the years because of the deception and betrayal in my family. I wondered, *How could we feel safe in a world with such deception?*

Just about the time I was done with my phone call, Tom arrived at my office. "Hey, you look down. What's up?"

"I just got a phone call and found out one of the couples I know at church are having problems. The husband is using pornography and prostitutes. Would you ever do that?"

Tom looked me square in the eyes, shook his head,

and said he would never do that "red light district stuff!"

Well, later that day, our marriage remodeling started when I found out that he had in fact been reading pornography. I discovered it when I got the mail before he came home, just after we came back from lunch and he went to pick up the kids after school. I wasn't sure exactly what was in this tightly wrapped plastic package as I pulled it out of the mailbox, but I knew it was something along those lines.

As I pondered what to do, I heard, "Put it in the drawer where the mail usually goes. Let it go for now and take a nap." So I did. When I got up, Tom was in an angry and defensive state. I asked him what wrong, only to hear some excuse about the kids and their so-called annoying behavior.

"Tom," I said, "the kids are doing just fine. What seems to really be the problem?"

Finally, he admitted to getting "one of those magazines" in the mail. He was showing a lot of anger and disgust as he continued to plead with me that it wasn't his fault, that he had cancelled his subscription almost a year ago. By this point he was in a state of complete panic and anger. The more he expressed his anger at "never being able to get away from his past," the more I grew concerned. Had he taken responsibility and repented, I would've felt safer. But his defensiveness felt like a cover-up to me.

Is it possible there is more to this? I wondered. I couldn't help but wonder after the morning phone call and after uncovering the secret of my childhood. For days, I tried to discuss the issue with Tom.

Finally, he admitted to using pornography at times when we were disconnected. I felt hurt and betrayed, somewhat from the use of the pornography, but more so from the deception. This was hitting me at the core. *Was the man I married capable of sneaking and lying like my birth father did to his wife, or the man at church with his wife? If he were using pornography after only three months of marriage, what would he be doing in three years?*

I wondered, *Why is this happening to me again? It's my worst nightmare come true!* Even more so, I wondered if I, alone, could ever be enough to satisfy him. I was already feeling like I was giving more than I had to give.

For the next month, we fought about it a lot. The more I tried to talk to him about it, the more we fought. Finally, I couldn't take it anymore. How was I to work through my fear and the problem if we couldn't discuss it? Yet, I knew it was no longer open communication at this point, although we were communicating. Our defenses were up like a wall surrounding the same hearts that once dreamed of the connection they could find in each other. After a few months, I decided to move out into the vacant, unsold condo that seemed like it was now waiting for me as a refuge.

We tried to save our marriage for months afterwards by going to counseling and doing whatever we thought would make it work. But the oddest thing happened: life didn't seem like it was supporting our efforts. It seemed as though wherever or to whomever we turned didn't work out. We tried counseling, only to find that our counselor had been fired after four weeks. Tom's doctor put him on an anti-depressant, thinking that the medication would help. We found out that he was actually manic-depressive and the antidepressant made the manic part worse.

In Tom's manic state, he was calling me constantly at the condo, giving me no space to deal with my pain and confusion. It wasn't so much what he was saying, it was his constant nonstop phone calls and need for answers that was getting to me. When I didn't know how I felt or couldn't give him what he needed, he would do something impulsive to get attention or soothe himself.

I wondered, *Who is this madman?* I couldn't seem to

resist the temptation to judge, *He's crazy.* In addition, I was judging myself. *Maybe I don't know him as well as I thought I did.* Either way, the fact was, it was what it was . . . and I didn't like it. I felt terrified.

Fear made me want to protect myself and isolate from Tom even more. As I withdrew, he went deeper into another reactive pattern. This time it was a flight pattern. He filed for divorce.

Just about the time Tom filed for divorce, an old boyfriend named John contacted me and told me he was going to be in town for the day. I decided to go to lunch with him to tell him I was married and let him know what was going on. To be perfectly honest, part of me did that out of my own reactive pattern of wanting to fight back. In my hurt, I wanted my actions to say to Tom, "How dare you badger me with your calls and file for divorce. Now I'll do want I want. You're not in control of me."

Needless to say, the "dance" didn't stop there. It didn't take long before Tom turned to another woman to soothe his pain. Although he denied his involvement, I knew. We always know, because things change when that happens.

11

"The Courage to Forgive the "Unforgivable"

In order to cope with the stresses in my life, I sought counsel from three main sources: a spiritual advisor, a psychologist, and my spiritual fellowship group, which met once a week to do a bible study on the Fruit of the Spirit. I decided I was sick of the craziness and wanted to learn how I might be co-creating the "dance" with Tom, instead of creating the love I so much desired. The common themes I took from all three resources were patience, kindness, forgiveness, trust, openness, and love–always with the intention of honoring God and viewing specific circumstances as a chance for the soul to grow.

It was hard to embody these qualities, especially when I was sure by now that my marriage was over. How could I trust a man who had looked me in the eyes and lied, eventually acted out impulsively, filed for divorce, and had an intimate relationship with another woman during this time? These were my "not" goals; I would absolutely not put up with these things!

Yet, I was being advised to stay open and embrace this, my worst nightmare. What did that mean exactly? Whatever it was, at this level, it was new to me!

Although I'd grown emotionally and spiritually over the past several years, I was using my newly acquired knowledge and skills to maintain my comfort zone. Could I now die to what I believed was my own comfort and safety and instead trust God? Could I stay open to the relationship with Tom if I believed it was for the ultimate growth of each of our souls? Could I give up the notion that it would somehow make me a doormat if I just trusted and allowed, a day at a time? Could I trust in God to keep me safe even when the circumstances looked bad and harmful to me? These were all the new questions I was wrestling with, as I faced this difficult situation.

As I was expanding out of my comfort zone, the tension in my body increased. A friend, going through a similar tough time with her son, suggested that I attend a yoga class that she found helpful in keeping centered. So I did. After an hour of stretching, the yoga teacher had us do a quiet meditation in which she had us visualize something that we felt was important for us to manifest in our life. I saw my heart enlarging inside my chest, as all the energy around it grew. Then, she asked for us to be still and breathe deeply. After several minutes, she asked us to look to the right in the mind's eye and see what appeared. I saw John, the former boyfriend with whom I'd had lunch right after Tom filed for divorce, and who had begun writing to me recently. My first reaction was to panic and push him away. Then, the instructor guided us to look to the left in the mind's eye and told us to notice what was there. I saw Tom. He had his arms crossed and wore a scornful look on his face. I reached out to him, but he wouldn't receive my affection.

As we were instructed to breathe more deeply, another vision came to me. I was sitting at a table with a man. He had no head or face. I was to the right of him and he to my left, as we were collaborating and discussing plans and finances. I couldn't tell who the man was, but one thing was evident: the connection was one of love and openness. It sure felt good! Although the outcome of my life was still ambiguous, I knew that this vision was there to give me hope while I was journeying down a very difficult and dark path.

As I continued to ponder my part in the relationship with Tom, and the lessons I was supposed to learn, our divorce proceedings were continuing. Finally, one day, while I was shopping, I experienced a big shift in my perspective. It wasn't until I sought out the truth about my life and my marriage with all my heart, that truth would appear. In order for me to change the patterns that had such a stronghold on me, I needed to be completely willing to receive truth and love from something bigger than me.

I'll never forget it. It was shortly after Thanksgiving. I was in Chicago with my oldest daughter who was now 21 years old. We were celebrating her 21st birthday and my 44th birthday. We did this by doing our traditional Christmas shopping weekend adventure in Chicago. She'd asked if we could go to Victoria's Secret in the Water Tower. As we entered the store, it occurred to me that this was the place I'd been the previous year to purchase my honeymoon lingerie. It also occurred to me that the first time I was married I had been my daughter's age: 21.

I thought about the great anticipation I felt the day I purchased every item for Tom's and my wedding. Deep sadness came over me as I went back over the disappointments of the last year. I sat still and pondered what had happened. I so wanted to manifest a good marriage and do heart and soul work through my business. Yet, I felt powerless in my ability to do what I wanted most.

As I sat in the chair, still waiting for Lisa to finish looking around, I surrendered the notion that I could ever create on my own the kind of marriage and work my heart desired. My self-protected heart had such a grip on me. I asked God and the Holy Spirit to show me, "What went wrong?"

That day in Chicago, I received the answer with grace, love, and gratitude. I felt like I died and went to heaven and saw my life from God's point of view. He showed me the dance I was in. I no longer saw my life as something that was happening to me, rather as something I could make happen, if only I could live it by faith. Faith was trusting first in God's love for me, and believing that He was ultimately in control, even if it didn't appear that way. My job was to be curious and to be in continual dialogue with Him, asking: What is the lesson here? What would You have me do or say? In order to do that, I had to embrace a love in something bigger than myself.

Now, I could see how, in a state of fear and judgment, I chose controlling and self-protection over trusting and allowing. The other option would be to connect with my Highest Self, God, and the Holy Spirit before I ever spoke or did anything. In the past, the more I was afraid of being controlled, the more I controlled.

As I meditated on my relationship with my husband, it became clear that we were mirrors. The more my husband chose self-protection in his way, the more I chose self-protection in my way. Looking back, I did this because his choices were the same behaviors of deception and betrayal I'd experienced as a child, and they felt like salt in my wounds. Although I had stopped betraying and deceiving myself when I decided to find out the truth of my birth father, I still had a deeper wound to heal than trusting my intuition. The question my soul was crying out was: *Can I trust in the love of God no matter what the circumstances are?*

Then, I heard God respond in a still, small voice:

"You both want the relationship, yet are behaving from what you learned. The problem is that neither of you have chosen to come to me in your pain. I AM where you will find love first."

All I could think was, *WOW! Of course, Spirit knows that even though we've heard the truth most of us still have a very difficult time letting go of deeply ingrained patterns of behavior, even ones that are not good for us.*

It was true for me. But I made a decision on the spot to just be with this awareness so that it would penetrate my heart.

Later that day, I received one more message. It came to me through my younger daughter Alex when I returned home. She had bought me the Celine Dion Christmas CD for my birthday because she knew I liked to sing Christmas carols in the car when I took her to school. I played it right away. When I did, I discovered that there was going to be a bigger intention for me than merely enjoying the music. Listening to the music and words from Dion's song "The Prayer" reinforced my awareness of the shift I needed to make in my life. God's message to me went from being head-knowledge to heart-knowledge. I could feel throughout my whole body the ways I needed to be different so that I could truly manifest my heart and soul's desire in every area of my life.

Love, gratitude, and openness filled me. The song made me realize that love, protection, wisdom, and power were always available to me, if I chose to access them. I especially liked the words in the beginning of the song. It's starts out with Dion singing and asking God to watch over us. She also prays, as she sings, for guidance and wisdom. Then she goes on to remind us that this needs to be our prayer, especially when others and we are lost. Then the listener gets to experience her heartfelt confidence as she sings about how she believes that God can lead us to a safe place and give us the grace we need on our journey, even when it is difficult.

As I played the song over and over again, my heart was riveted with both joy and sorrow. I was aware that I wasn't asking God with all my heart to show me wisdom and give me strength as I faced the difficult situations over the last year. I could also see how I was relying on my plans, my strategies, and my intuition, instead of His power. It seemed as though I kept hearing the same message over and over again from people, experts I sought out, and sometimes out of nowhere. I knew that God was trying to get my attention to let me know my next lesson was on love. I kept hearing,

"It's all about how deeply you love."

Could I forgive and love someone under these circumstances? I knew the answer was: "Not in my power alone." I decided that I wanted to learn a new way to love unconditionally and for the Highest Good of All.

Looking back, as I saw all the pieces to the puzzle of my life, I could see why God had allowed everything to unfold as it did. Nothing I experienced was wasted. Life was supporting me all along. It just didn't appear that way at first because I was only open to seeing love in the ways I expected it. In actuality, Tom and I were both being supported in "removing the blocks that kept us from loving each other completely," which had been our prayer before our marriage! We had to face our personal demons in order to cast them away. How might we have done things differently if we'd known our patterns of reaction sooner? I felt humbled.

Simple awareness was replaced by deep repentance. I felt deep sorrow as I realized the opportunities I'd missed to truly love. Out of my pride, I chose fear and self-protection. Trusting in my intuition alone would not work if I were using it out of fear. I had to surrender to God, and then my inner wisdom would guide me truthfully. As I integrated these lessons, the tears flowed on and off for almost a week. My heart hadn't felt this open since I attended Leo Buscaglia's seminar on the night my dad died.

After releasing all the sadness and sorrow for my part in the dance of fear, judgment, and control, I felt renewed. Gratitude of great magnitude took over my whole being. I felt empowered by a radiant love within, as

I now understood the new choice I could make in my very difficult situation: to love. What would that look like exactly? In order to find out, I had to be willing to be flexible and to not believe I knew the answer until I asked in the moment. Even more so, I had to know that I could trust God to love me, no matter what the circumstances might look like or what the outcome might be. Only then, could I freely choose what behaviors I needed to in the moment to be a vessel of love, as I was guided.

Tom and I were merely days away from our divorce court date when the voice within instructed me to call him and apologize for my part in our "dance." My intention was simply to share that I felt sad that it didn't work out between us. I also wanted him to know that our relationship had actually been quite healing for me, even though it didn't have the outcome I'd imagined.

When I reached him on the phone, after initial reluctance, he matched my openness. Not only did he apologize for his deception, he also apologized for badgering me and filing for divorce. In addition, he explained how promiscuity was a misguided means of securing love and connection. Although I appreciated his apology, I still struggled with wanting perfection in our relationship even more than honesty. Yet, he continued. He shared that he'd slept with two other women during our separation and what he was feeling when he made those choices: insecurity, misguided love, low self-esteem, hurt, loneliness, desperation, and more.

Suddenly I had compassion for all the people in my life who had similar experiences. As much as I was sad, scared, hurt, and angry, I could understand the temptation. I had made that choice when I was separated from my first husband, too, when I became sexually involved with Gary. I understood how Richard, my mother, and Tom could feel so needy for something outside of themselves to try to fill their emptiness. I had, at one time, felt that lost and empty too. I wondered, *How would I have wanted Steve to respond in "love" to me?* I also felt compassion for Steve, and for Richard's wife: it must have been difficult to trust someone after infidelity occurred, even if it was during separation. Yet, although I could forgive and feel compassion, I still was not sure I wanted to be in a relationship with someone I wasn't sure I could trust.

Is this conversation what emotional intimacy is all about? I wondered.

It was difficult for me to hear how he'd been with other women to soothe his pain during the time we were separated. However, as I faced my biggest nightmare, I sensed my freedom from the bondage of my fear. I had realized my tendency in the past to go into a victim mentality around the issue of betrayal. I wasn't as tempted to blame him as I would have been in the past. Nonetheless, the familiar urge was there. I asked God to help me stay open and be a vessel of love. Until the phone call ended, I breathed through the pain. I was beginning to feel my transformation.

Later that night, going to God for guidance and strength helped me face my disappointment about Tom's honest confession of his tendency towards promiscuity as a way to soothe his pain. With all my heart, I asked God, "What am I supposed to learn from this?"

In response, I heard:

"No sin is greater than the other. You both are forgiven."

12

The Courage to Live
a Life of Love

Although I certainly would not have written the first year of my marriage in the way that it played out, I was grateful for the lessons I learned on love. Looking deeper beyond my circumstances, I knew the lesson: How might we all think, feel, and behave so that we can be vessels of love and enthusiasm even in the most difficult situations? In Ancient Greek, *enthusiasm* means "God within." This question became the most important in my life.

The following summer we decided to cancel the divorce we had pending to see if we could reconcile our marriage. We sold the condo and the home we had originally bought and found another home in the area that seemed to meet our needs better. As we moved our furniture out, I walked around the house one final time before the movers drove away. Entering the empty laundry room, I was reminded of the dream I had just prior to seeing the house for the first time. The feelings in the dream came back to me. *Oh my gosh,* I thought. *It was a precognitive dream. All of this was my destiny.* Yet I wondered, *what would my life have looked like if I would've slowed down that day and honored the precognitive vision and feelings?* I knew I had grown when I could recognize this oversight and still give myself grace and love in the place I was in my journey at the time.

As the next month unfolded, we were again busy with unpacking and re-decorating a new house to make it our home. Tom was in the remodeling business and enjoyed this type of work. So did I. But, about a month after we moved, we had to face issues of a blended family together again. Addressing issues, openly discussing our feelings and needs, agreeing to a plan and following through were difficult for us to do together. Now the day-to-day issues of marriage and a blended family were right there for us to deal with regularly. On top of our own adjustment, Tom's ex-wife decided to serve him with a court order regarding placement issues the day we moved in.

Although pornography and promiscuity were no longer the big issues, I was able to see that what was at the "tip of the iceberg" was our inability to bring God into the everyday stresses of our lives. The new challenge was no longer surrendering the big things, listening to intuition, or forgiveness. The new lesson was to learn to trust and love by having a very personal relationship with God, each and every moment. In order to do this, we had to surrender and listen to Him. Only then could we have the courage to live a life of faith and love. The new question on my heart was, "How do we bring God into the littlest things?"

Isn't it amazing that when we seek truth with all our heart we will find it? The biggest truth I learned was: Don't make decisions out of fear; make choices out of love.

In order to bring God into the littlest things, I had to be self-aware when I was feeling fear versus love. When I was feeling fear, I had to be willing to admit my powerlessness in my situation. If I didn't, all of my actions would be a "counterfeit love." My choices, if made out of fear, would have an ulterior motive: safety and comfort. But what would those behavior choices look like if they were made in love?

I was learning that our decisions are never about the decision itself, they're about the intention behind the decision. We need to ask God and ourselves: Am I making this decision out of fear or love? He will help us to become more self-aware. Once we are more conscious, our next question is, How might I be a vessel of love in this situation?

Being open to God's leading can often bring us to choices that we otherwise would not make on our own. Sometimes those choices create great discomfort for a while for someone else or for us. As a result, it can bring up lots of sadness, fear, and anger that need to be healed and released. If we make choices so that others or ourselves do not feel those "uncomfortable" feelings, we could possibly be choosing unloving behaviors. This was a new lesson I was learning: Sometimes we are asked to allow for pain, so that there is an opportunity for gain on a heart and soul level.

As I began to trust in a love that was bigger than myself, I felt more confidence in making choices in my life that were loving to myself and others on a soul level. The most difficult part of this equation for me was still including my needs and feelings in the daily moments.

I had a "not" goal that I had vowed to achieve as a child. I did not want to be selfish like my mother. This was the area of my life that I was healing. I realized the people I was struggling with the most were probably learning the opposite lesson: How might they include others in their equation of love, instead of only thinking of themselves? Both dynamics were mirrors of the same problem; two ends of a spectrum based on fear and not love. One end was fear of not loving enough; the other end was fear of loving too much. Both ends of the dynamic offered an opportunity first to release the fear and powerlessness to God, and then to ask Him to show the path of love.

Making this shift, my life began to look imperfect and out of control from my earthly point of view. This was because I was stretching my comfort zone. I was back in the unknown once again. As I stopped accommodating others in order to try to control their responses, I was left with my feelings of fear and sadness. Believing I could control "love" was an illusion I had to release.

As I was practicing this lesson with the people that were dearest to my heart, I felt a lot of resistance. My mother and Tom in particular became more angry, critical, and distant as I set more boundaries and limitations with them. I felt challenged as I claimed my feelings, needs, courage, truth, and goals in my life in the day-to-day moments. I knew this experience was allowed to strengthen me. There was no doubt in my mind that, in part, the lessons I would learn in my reconciliation with Tom would include learning to love myself in the everyday moments and decisions. This is where I lost my connection in my first two marriages. Now I had a chance to do it differently. In order to make this shift, I would have to draw closer to God for love, guidance, courage, and truth in the midst of this uncertainty. Learning what it means to "trust Him in the littlest things" would be my next lesson in my journey of emotional and spiritual growth.

In order to make the behavior changes I needed to make, I needed to trust God more. How would I do that? Then it occurred to me: I had to reconcile my feelings about Him, to Him. This required complete and ruthless honesty. I had to ask God: Why did you allow catastrophic things to occur in my life? Even more so, I needed to know: Where were you in the day-to-day moments when I felt so alone?

I was beginning to realize that my perspective of God came from my experience with my parents. I only knew how to try to please my parents. I didn't know how to connect with them authentically and how to receive emotional nurture from them.

As a child, I was conditioned to think about everyone else's needs because no one had the time or capacity to care for mine. Thus, I was unaware of my feelings or how to trust God's love in the "littlest things." It wasn't that God wasn't meeting my needs, I simply was not aware of my needs or His traffic signals within me that said,

"Yield," "Slow down," "Proceed with caution," and, "Stop!" I wasn't open and aware because I didn't ask, trust, and allow for Him to speak to me regarding choices I could make that would be loving to others and myself.

Without being aware of God's love first, it was difficult for me to love others and myself. This was especially difficult in the midst of little disappointments and betrayals. Those situations would trigger my deeper belief that God was not watching over me and protecting me. It would also trigger my deepest sadness, hurt, and anger that were still waiting to be healed from the daily disappointments of my childhood.

One day, I was ready to find out, "Was God really different than my parents?" It was a few months after Tom and I had stopped our divorce proceedings and bought our new house. Once again, we were struggling with the same adjustment pains regarding collaborative decisions. Tom and I had just had a big blowout.

This time I asked God to come into the conflict resolution with me. This was one of the first times I invited God into my healing process right from the beginning, and when I did . . . I did in a big way. I let Him have it! I gave Him all of my anger, all of my disappointment, and all of my despair! I demanded, "Show me the love in this! I'm being so faithful to you and yet life is so hard!" And, there, in the center of my pain, He met me.

It's not that I had never felt a connection with Him before–I had. For instance: my spiritual awakening 15 years earlier, when I saw the cross on my church's lawn, which is what Christians call a "born-again" experience. Another connection occurred when I found out about my birth father and forgave my mother. I'd also felt a deep connection when Tom and I reconciled and I realized that being in God's Love and Spirit was more important to me than being self-protecting.

But, this time, I got ruthlessly honest with Him. I

said, "Hey what about me?" I also told him what I really thought about Him: He wasn't doing His job! Surprisingly, I could sense that He loved it. This was the first time anyone had ever been big enough to handle my intensity.

It wasn't until I had let it all out that I heard His loving voice:

> "I know that life didn't turn out exactly as you wished. I know you wished your mother had been more present and emotionally available. I know you wished your dad had never died. I know you wished that uncovering the secret had healed your relationship with your mother. I know you wished that marriage were the promise of 'happily ever after.' But I have something better for you than those dreams. Step back for a moment. You'll see that I gave you your deepest heart and soul's desire. Love was always present in ME. It just doesn't always come wrapped up like you expect. Trust in me with all your heart and I will direct your path."

I thought about that for a minute. I thought back to all the big and little hurts and disappointments. I thought about how I was attached to outcomes. That it was the attachment to what I thought was "the ideal way of being happy and loved" that caused me pain when it didn't happen that way. Within those circumstances were loving-lessons I learned that helped me grow emotionally and spiritually. God was the loving parent, making decisions for my life for my Highest Good.

Looking back, I could see that I was still "pulling up my bootstraps" and trying to be a good Christian through it all. Yet, deep down inside, I was having another experience. Being authentic with God helped me transmute my earthly perspective, release my ego's needs and feelings, and open myself up to His perspective and love.

He was the ultimate role model of "trusting and allowing." How wonderful it was to have the One-Minute Meditation to rely on, and also to have a One-Minute Wrestling Match with God to clear the deck in each moment. Through emotionally authentic connection, I could be transformed into His likeness as I faced everyday decisions in each moment. Through connection with God, I could find courage and truth that allows His higher perspective and love to flow through my life.

By virtue of this new desire, I was transforming from my own personal concerns to those of God. I was giving up the personal "*I am* going to do this or that," and replacing it with my desire to please the "Great I AM." This is how the Bible refers to God. For a motivational teacher who formerly believed in personal empowerment, this was a big shift.

Now I could see that the perfect balance of empowerment was first to be aware of difficult situations and people and then to invite God into our emotional responses and patterns as they were happening in the moment. That balance would keep us open and responsible, while surrendering to God's power. Then we could ask Him to help us choose the most loving statements and actions that He wants instilled on our hearts. When we do this, we have less fear in the moment and fewer regrets because we are filled with His loving nourishment no matter what the circumstances. With this process, we are tapping into the secret to "I AM."

Day-to-day chronic stresses give us an opportunity to make a choice as we face the fork in the road. Will we choose: What's in it for me? Make me feel important? Or will we choose: Show me what is for the Highest Good of All! I AM Yours!

Yet, when we live fast paced lives of pressure,

disconnection, and control for too long, we can easily forget that we need God. It helps to view daily difficulties as an opportunity for an act of love! They allow us to choose: Who's in control of my life? Who will I serve—myself, someone else, or God? We need to ask Him what love would look like in our situation.

The Fourth Secret is to acknowledge that difficult situations and lessons will always appear in order to remind us to embrace a love in something bigger than ourselves. How we choose to respond in difficult situations is what really counts. We can ignore the guidance we receive, play the victim, persecute others or ourselves, and keep repeating patterns; or we can choose to act differently. A powerful option is to trust in the love of God and the Holy Spirit for truth, guidance, strength, and love. When we make this choice, then we are truly living in the "I AM'" presence. God affords us capabilities, confidence, and love beyond our own means.

When we discover the secret to "I AM," it doesn't mean we always live in complete confidence and trust that we're loved by God. However, once we've felt the deep knowing that we do have everything we need to get where we need to go, we become more conscious. We grow increasingly aware of when we're carrying anxiety and self-doubt, as a result of believing otherwise. The Fourth Secret equips us to recognize that our problems stem from fear, judgment, and control rather than our circumstances. Thus, we're more able to take responsibility to get back on track by making the preferred choice to surrender, trust, and allow.

This new way of being allows us to feel secure in very uncertain and difficult times. Instead of judging circumstances as "good" or "bad," "right" or "wrong," we can ask, "Show me the love in this." By having the courage to ask, we can get the reassurance we need and therefore be reminded that a powerful force bigger than us is really in control of everything, and for the Highest

Good of All.

In addition to these lessons having a positive impact on healing my past and learning to trust God, I was amazed to see the effect that opening my heart to God had on my relationships and my career. Now, when I want to do His will more than my own, the outcome doesn't matter as much as enjoying the journey. I have changed directions in both my personal and professional lives. Instead of being overly aware of what others want, I ask, "What is Your will for me right now, God?"

Some of His answers haven't produced the results I would've liked immediately. But I trust and have courage because I know that I am focused on His truth and love. The biggest change I can see in the immediate moment is that, because I believe I am loved first by Him, I am able to live with my heart wide open. That's a big enough payoff for me.

As I think about this new way of being an open vessel of love, I think about Nelson Mandela's 1994 inaugural speech when he became President of South Africa. He directly quoted Marianne Williamson's book entitled *The Return to Love*. Each time I read the message, I feel inspired to manifest the glory of God and become all I can be. It speaks of how our worst fear is our power. It addresses how we are afraid to be our best selves, in fear that this might intimidate, alienate, offend, or make someone else feel insecure. But then it goes on to say that overcoming these fears, finding our courage and our connection with God is our ultimate purpose. We are all supposed to be vessels of love on this earth, and not to "play weak" in order to give instant soothing to others, or to control the outcome. She continues by reminding us that as we embrace our "Big Selves" we glorify God and help others to do the same.

I am grateful for the journey to understand the secret to the "I AM" presence in my life. It taught me a new way of being with myself, others, and God as I move towards my dreams and goals.

Looking back on the profound moments of my life, I am incredibly moved by the memory of hearing Leo Buscaglia speak. I remember how within I heard: "Someday, you too will have a message on love." Maybe that still, small voice was trying to tell me about the message I finally received on where to get real love. In any case, it's certain: One must be the student before becoming the teacher. For all my experiences, I AM grateful, as it helped me to live life with my heart wide open.

Lessons and Wisdom:

*Tips for Working with
the Four Secrets*

Lessons and Wisdom

As I was wrapping up the final editing of this book, I asked God and my intuition: Is there anything else you would like me to share? I AM yours! Practicing the same techniques I've described elsewhere, I surrendered, trusting and allowing that if there were anything more the answer would come to me in perfect timing. That night, just before bed, I grabbed my latest edition of O magazine. Flipping through the pages, a perfume ad practically jumped out at me. Its words read: In the eye of the storm I AM still.

Oneness. We are all more alike than we may realize. Although there are surface differences, in many ways we share experiences. The names of the players and the details of our circumstances vary, yet the story is the same. Whether we are talking about my story or your story, underneath it, our hearts and souls are learning identical lessons on love.

As I thought about the new fragrance, Still, which I'd seen advertised, I remembered a Bible verse I'd hand-painted above the sink in the kitchen of my house: Be still and know I AM God. (Psalm 46:10). *Hmm . . . Isn't that interesting? Isn't that what life is really all about?*

Whether we are currently facing a death, a divorce, a difficult relationship, unemployment, a health issue, an injury, a deep betrayal, a big change, a broken dream, or life is currently more than we expected, realizing that there are lessons and blessings in the situation makes us grateful and helps us accept that we are loved.

There is great freedom in the mindset of loving gratitude. When we say to ourselves, "I AM no longer taking things personally," we can be grateful for others and their openness. When we believe, "I AM defined by my choices, not by the choices others make," we can be grateful for the strength of our inner connection. When we know with all our heart that "I AM love," we are grateful because we feel complete with or without a relationship. When we trust that "I AM enough," we move toward our goals with gratitude and inner peace. Likewise, of course, when we claim, "I AM Yours God," we automatically feel fulfilled, because we're connected with the great "I AM."

In this section of the book, I'll revisit elements of my story and explain the techniques I was using to help myself so that you can apply them in your own life. Because I believe in the deepest part of my heart and soul that my story contains universal lessons, I plan to share the lessons I learned more generally.

Tips for the First Secret: How Might I Embrace My Uniqueness?

People ask me how I "knew" that I had a different birth father, while my brother and other family members didn't know. That's been a difficult question for me to answer. In part, I think it was just my destiny to know and my purpose to share my story with others. My brother and others have different life paths, which each will have to discover by asking themselves: How might I utilize this experience for the Highest Good of All? What is my lesson? How might I create purpose from the pain?

I struggled with self-doubt throughout much of my life because I didn't embrace my unique quality of intuition. I had heard and believed too many shaming remarks, like, "It's just your imagination." As a result, I found it difficult to embrace my perceptions, and claim them as acceptable and appropriate even when others were offended by my truth.

When we don't unconditionally accept who we are in our essence and take other people's comments personally, we experience self-doubt.

The First Secret taught me to honor and embrace my truth regardless of seeking approval, affirmation, or a specific outcome. "Happily ever after" is an illusion I've had to let go. I've also had to learn how to slow down and do what I needed to feel completely connected to myself in the moment, even if it meant that I had to travel down the road of joy, love, truth, and peace alone.

Like most people, when I used to be more disconnected from my emotions and my intuition, I would often chose a "flight or flight" pattern of relating. Although in a heightened state of anxiety I was very emotional, I wasn't integrated enough to explore and embrace the wisdom of my emotions.

Whenever people swing from "fight" to "flight," they're experiencing an opportunity for healing. But it only takes place, if they're willing to explore their self-doubt. For me, getting to the point of "I've had it!" often had to do with my negative judgment against others and myself for not being "in-tune." I didn't believe I was appropriately conscious or connected within in the moment.

It wasn't until I could transmute my judgment towards people who were in denial that I finally got a taste of compassion. Compassion arose in me when I became curious, *Hmm . . . Why do people choose not to know?* Then, I remembered . . . I myself wasn't ready to know the entire truth about my parentage until I was almost 33 years old. I was more focused on connecting with others than myself. With that reminder, I realized that we could all only make choices to see truth when we felt equipped to do so.

So that we can live a life of truth and awareness, we must cultivate grace and compassion for others and ourselves. We are all working through our own illusions and messages of fear and self-doubt.

One way we can recognize self-doubt is by noticing the negative statements we say to ourselves. The psychological term for this is cognitive self-awareness. For me, self-doubt often sounded like, "What's wrong with me . . . Why doesn't this big elephant under the carpet bother anyone else?" "Maybe I expect too much!" and "I'm not easy-going enough!"

What does self-doubt sound like for you? Does it say:
- ❖ "You'll never amount to anything!"
- ❖ "If they only knew me they would judge me!"
- ❖ "I'll never be able to find the relationship or career I really want!"
- ❖ "I'm not qualified enough to go after my dream!" or,
- ❖ "I'll never be able to lose weight," and so on?

Begin paying attention to the messages of your self-doubt, as they keep you from embracing your uniqueness.

As I realized my tendency to treat myself in such an unloving way, my life began to change because I started embracing my unique qualities. Today, I recognize self-doubt by observing not only my thoughts, but also the emotional energy in my body. Rather than judging the experience I'm having, I simply explore it by asking, *Hmm . . . Isn't that interesting? I wonder what the self-doubt is about?* Then, *What is real and true here? How does my body feel–relaxed, tight, twitchy, sleepy, and so on?*

Affirming my sense of reality in the midst of someone else's denial can also prove helpful. An affirmation such as "My heart is open to truth and love, and I deliver it with grace and ease," can keep me grounded and connected within, instead of taking on someone else's fear.

Learning to notice, explore, and heal self-doubt as it comes up has been one of the biggest lessons that

I've learned. Taking responsibility to do this moment-to-moment has helped me manifest the life I want to have. It has also helped me not to become complacent. As I stretch to become all that I can be, I often re-visit self-doubt and have to go through this process again.

One of the other ways that we can heal self-doubt and embrace our uniqueness is to notice when we feel confusion. We feel confusion when the messages we're getting seem incongruent. If a person's words say one thing while his or her body language and tone of voice are communicating something else, we feel confused. In such cases, always pay more attention to the tone of voice and the body language than the actual words, as research has shown that they account for about 90 percent of the message.

We also feel confusion when we don't take the time to explore and embrace what we uniquely want. In my case, this was true when it came to relationships with men. Because my mother was very opinionated regarding what kind of guy would be best for me, I wasn't given a blank piece of paper on which to create my own vision. Instead, I was handed a script of how to be and whom to choose.

On the other hand, when it came to my career, I was told, "You can be anything you want to be. You could even be President of the United States if you wanted!" This gave me the courage to explore "Who am I and what do I want to be when I grow up?" It's not to say that I never experienced self-doubt in my career. I have and do. The difference is that I can more easily identify what I'm feeling and need to get over my confusion and self-doubt in my career.

When we ask the question, "Who am I anyway?" we automatically go into a process of exploration. In order to explore our uniqueness, we need to ask questions like, "Okay then, what do I want?" Using the term "How might I . . . ? helps us to trigger possibilities.

As my journey of self-awareness progressed, I began to ask questions, such as:

❖ "How might I enjoy being alone?"
❖ "How might I create an enjoyable, loving relationship?"
❖ "How might I allow myself and others to be who they are and where they are in their journeys?"
❖ "How might I be authentic in my choices, while still embracing my husband's needs and feelings?"
❖ "How might I stay connected with my truth and allow others to see and know what they need to know?"

These types of questions can be helpful in getting clear about what we want, especially if we have what's called "double-minded thinking." Double-minded thinking is when we want one aspect of something but not another aspect that we perceive we must have if we are to have the other. For example, I want to expand my business but I don't want to go in debt. Therefore, my double-mind thinks "I want to expand/I don't want to expand." This paralyzes me. In order not to experience double-minded thinking, I need to ask, "Okay, how might I expand my business and simultaneously remain debt-free?"

Exploring who we are, and what we want and need is different than knowing what we don't want. "Not" goals cannot help us embrace our uniqueness. They tell us what we are avoiding, rather than what we want to create and attract.

I had many "not" goals growing up. I did not want to be alone. I did not want to get a divorce. I did not want to be judged. I did not want to have a bad relationship with my mother or husband. I did not want to lose my independence even though I was married. I did not want to lose my truth in the midst of someone else's strong perspective or opinion.

How would I ultimately begin to get what I wanted so

that I could truly embrace my uniqueness? It simply came down to recognizing my self-doubt and exploring what it was that I truly needed and wanted.

Tips for the Second Secret: How Might I Embrace the Unknown?

The Second Secret was examining how I typically reacted when faced with unknown situations. The first catastrophic situation in my life was the death of my father at age 18. This threw me into the unknown in a big way. From that, I learned what hopelessness looks and feels like.

Because I wasn't ready for the unknown, I established a "flight" pattern of running from my emotions, as well as a "fight" pattern of trying to bring his essence back into my life through my relationships with other men. Although it was painful to go through divorce to learn the lesson, I realized that if I could embrace the unknown without judgment or expectations, I could experience life with fewer detours and less pain.

Due to the sudden disappointment of my father's death, I struggled my whole life with "surprising news." This didn't change until someone significant in my life suggested, "Stop being surprised all the time. Life is full of surprises. That's just how it is!" The awareness that the unknown always exists was freeing to me. Although it may not sound profound to you, the concept gave me a new way to "frame" surprising news.

These days, when I get bad news, I'm much more able to say, "Okay, it is what it is, so I can stop pretending otherwise or wishing that it wasn't true." Now, the question I ask myself is, "How might I deal with this piece of news?" My new way of thinking helps me from adopting one of two other typical, and extreme, thought patterns: "doom and gloom" or "Pollyanna positive." On gloomy days, I used to despair, "I'll never find out who my birth father is!" or "Life will be so hard and lonely without Dad. I have no one else to turn to!" On Pollyanna days, I would say peppy things to myself like, "Everything is fine!" even though deep down I felt sad and hopeless.

What I learned was that curiosity is the key to handling the unknown. Instead of hoping a situation is different or feeling hopeless, curiosity unlocks our abilities to surrender, to be open, to trust, and to allow for life to unfold as it needs to unfold for the Highest Good of All of us.

In the face of the unknown, when I stopped judging things as good or bad, right or wrong, I could simply get curious and say, *Hmm . . . Isn't that interesting? I wonder . . . now what?* Such phrases became a powerful means of keeping me aligned with the adventure of life instead of futilely demanding life to change to be what I thought it ought to be. That's not to say that, at times, it wasn't a struggle. Sometimes my anxiety and fear desperately wanted an answer NOW. I so wanted life to meet my expectations. That was part of my lesson too: to learn to be in the present moment, curious and asking, instead of waiting and holding my breath.

For me, the sign that I was surrendering was when I stopped strategizing, or trying to figure things out in the Ben Franklin method of examining the pros and cons of certain actions and outcomes. Another sign was that I stopped being angry that life hadn't gone my way. When I could simply ask a question and let it go, get on with my life, and know that I would know in perfect timing–when I was supposed to know–I could feel peace in the unknown.

Looking back on my journey, you can see that the unknown held many lessons for me. One of them was to realize my fears, my attachments, and the myths I still believed about others and myself. When I would feel fear, loss, or shame, I had the opportunity to explore what they were trying to tell me.

For example, when my mother called me late at night, angry that I wanted to do DNA testing, I struggled with the fear: *What if I am wrong, and I put everyone through this?* I also struggled with loss, *What if my mother will never forgive me? And shame, Am I wrong to want to know the truth? Am I selfish?* Exploring those feelings and questions helped me not only to embrace the unknown situation, it helped me to explore my unknown self. Part of me was so disconnected from knowing how to love. I could only learn to love myself by being willing to embrace the unknown and my unique experience in it.

The unknown is where we find our courage. One of the ways we build courage is by asking questions about the unknown. When we ask, we open to truth rather than creating our own reality and establishing illusions in our mind. When we quickly fill in the blanks in the unknown situations, we're not being courageous; we're operating out of fear, judgment, and control.

In my journey, I was learning how to be in the unknown by connecting and having the courage to ask myself how I felt in a given situation. In addition, I was learning to have the courage to ask my intuition what was real and true? That took courage because I was giving up people pleasing. I no longer automatically agreed with others' senses of reality, perceptions, needs, and wants if they did not match my own. Instead, I was becoming more connected within and more authentic with others.

Having the courage to ask and listen within was scarier for me than to ask others direct questions. Honoring myself was a big part of the healing in my journey. What would be healing for you? Is it asking and listening within to your own truth, or is it asking and listening to others to be open to their truth? In either case, we are all called to honor each other.

The courage to ask is only effective when we've let go of our attachment to a specific outcome in a situation. If we don't want to hear the truth, we won't hear it from our intuition or from someone else, no matter how direct the message. That was the case for me during the ride in my dad's truck on that perfect 72-degree day when I asked him if he was my birth father. I only had the courage to ask because my heart was so wide open in the moment. The moment was all that mattered. The question wasn't pre-planned, it's just what came out of my mouth because I had the courage to let go of any planned outcome.

But when I "heard" the truth from my father's expression and from my intuition, the pain of my reaction made my heart shut down in fear once again. I wasn't ready to experience the loss of my dad. He had always provided me with a sense of safety and security.

What illusions of safety and security are you holding onto? Do you have a need to belong? A need for recognition? A need for pleasure and gratification? A need for soothing? A need for financial security? A need for material comfort? A need for physical pleasure? A need for your life to be organized? A need to have a plan you can count on? A need for predictability and consistency? A need for peaceful circumstances? A need for a job with purpose? A need for a job you enjoy? A need for a love relationship that makes you happy? A need for others to let you know about something? A need for others to behave in a specific way that you deem appropriate?

When we believe that we need anything that we perceive as being outside of us, we're attached to an illusion instead of the truth.

Here's a technique to help get in touch with the truth:
- ❖ If you have a need to belong, ask: Who am I?
- ❖ If you have a need for recognition, ask: How might I

love myself and stay connected within?

❖ If you have a need for pleasure and gratification, ask: How might I live with my heart wide open to life right now?

❖ If you have a need for soothing and comfort, ask: How might I nurture and love myself?

❖ If you need financial security, ask: How might I fully recognize and appreciate the abundance of beauty around me and within me each day?

❖ If your need is for material comfort, ask: How might I tap into the comfort of my spirit within?

❖ If your need is for physical pleasure and comfort, ask: How might I find a way to connect with my body?

❖ If you need your circumstances to be organized, ask: How might I feel more control within?

❖ If you need to have a plan you can count on, ask: How can I trust that this moment is all there really is?

❖ If you need predictability and consistency, ask: How can I enjoy the spontaneity, surprise, and blessings of this moment?

❖ If you need is peaceful circumstances, ask: How might I feel peace in the midst of chaos?

❖ If you need to have a job with purpose, ask: How might I be purposeful in the circumstances and job I have?

❖ If you need to enjoy your job, ask: How might I enjoy the responsibilities in my current life?

❖ If you need a love relationship that makes you happy, ask: How might I love the people in the relationships I am in?

❖ If you need others to let you know about something, ask: How might I trust my own knowing and myself?

❖ If you need others to behave in a specific way that you deem appropriate, ask: How might I give myself permission to be who I am?

See how this works? When we give up our illusions of safety and security and get curious instead, we can embrace and enjoy the unknown moments of our lives with more ease. We can do so, because we're admitting our self-doubt and feelings of powerlessness. Options in our situations that we couldn't see previously are revealed by identifying the source of our discomfort and then asking a possibility question triggered by the phrase, "How might I . . . ?"

The exercise on the previous page helps us realize that we're not dependent on outside circumstances to give us what we need. We can find all that we need within us, if we just ask.

Tips for the Third Secret: How Might I Embrace Intuitive Wisdom?

Embracing intuitive wisdom is another way we can empower ourselves in difficult and uncertain situations. There are two levels of intuition: retrieval intuition and direct knowing. As we develop personally and spiritually, we become more attuned to both types. Thus, we learn to trust ourselves and claim more of our power in the present moment. When we connect with intuitive wisdom we feel more courageous, clear, and peaceful.

Retrieval intuition relates to knowledge and experiences that we've stored in our brains. The more experiences we have in a given area of life, the more we can rely on retrieval intuition to guide us. In new situations, similar to past events, we simply know what to do. We can trust our gut, as some would say.

For most of my life, I had much stronger retrieval intuition in the area of business than I did as a woman in relationship with a man. Because my mother had her own small, home based business, and my aunt was the president of a college, tons of retrieval intuition is available to me as a businesswoman. I also have retrieval intuition because my degree is in Business and Communication.

On the other hand, because my mother was single and my aunt was a nun, I don't have many experiences or role models as a wife. Intuition in this area of my life comes to me through direct knowing, the second type of intuition, which is harder to trust at times. When we rely on direct knowing, we don't have any experiences to validate us. It's in such situations that we may struggle more with self-doubt, and also have opportunities to transmute the doubt and fear by connecting deeply within for the answers that are authentic for us.

This type of intuition is accessed through direct questions we ask our intuitive wisdom and God. It's not based on logic, reason, or experience. Wisdom just comes when we ask with all our heart, or, in other words, with our heart wide open. This is what is meant when in the Bible it says, "Trust in the Lord with all your heart, He will direct your paths." That means: Complete trust without fear. Although direct knowing is more difficult to trust at times than retrieval wisdom, when we do begin to trust ourselves in uncharted areas, we tend to feel a deeper connection within.

At the highest level, intuitive wisdom is God speaking to us. Some may say it is the Holy Spirit or the Divine. Although externally it may look as though my career has been more successful than my love life, I believe that God is more pleased with my progress in relationships. That area of my life is where I've learned, "Through my weakness, He is strong!"

Discovering my birth father came from direct knowing. I had to surrender completely and keep my heart open so that I could be guided to that truth. Part of my journey was letting go so that I could get on with life until the answer to that question came to me. In order to do so, I had to learn to trust in perfect timing. It was an adventure. My answer would sometimes come in a dream, while other times the answer came from a message I heard internally as a still, small voice, and still other times through conversations.

The idea of direct knowing is simply to receive your messages however they come to you.

When I picture the connection between the self, the intuition, and God, I picture it in the shape of an "L." I imagine energy coming down through the tops of our heads, and then flowing out through our hearts. In order to establish this connection, when we've decided to live in the "L" before we speak or act, we must first detach from other people or the situation we're in, and then connect by going within and asking a question.

Remember that we can only ask our intuition one simple question at a time. Once you have that question answered, another question may come up. That's great! Just continue to be curious and ask.

Notice that the way I am describing living in the "L"–the power of the connection is from the base of the stem of the "L" and continually moves upward for truth and love until we are clear and connected. Before we move outward to speak or take action, we wait to be sure that our intention is in love, for the Highest Good of All.

When we're in a reactive pattern we don't take time to visit the base of the "L"; we just quickly do or say something so that we can have the instant gratification of feeling in control of the situation. That's how we lose our center. It's an illusion that we can be in control in the first place!

In order to live in the "L," the energy of love, we can do the One-Minute Meditation process. I teach this technique in the workplace so that people won't lose their sense of balance and connection in the midst of the uncertainty and chaos they may experience.

When I was at my mother's house with my birth

father and my brother, I did a One-Minute Meditation to gather information. Although at the time I did it spontaneously, I have since identified the steps I went through to gain clarity.

The One-Minute Meditation works as follows:

First, prepare. Detach from the person you're with, or the situation you're in by saying: "Hmm...isn't that interesting, I wonder . . . (finish the sentence with whatever it is that you are wondering about)?" This puts you in a neutral, observant state of mind. Simply feel curious and observe the behaviors around you without judgment. We're being judgmental when we conclude someone or something is "good/bad" or "right/wrong."

Afterwards, connect with your intuitive wisdom by saying: "I am able to attract truth and wisdom in perfect timing." This opens you up to the guidance of your intuitive wisdom and connects you with your heart, which is where you know truth and love.

Continue to connect within by taking three deep, cleansing breaths. As you breathe in, picture yourself breathing in peace and love. As you exhale, picture yourself exhaling anxiety and fear.

Now that you're in a neutral and observant state of being, you're ready to do the Six-Point Check that follows:

First, notice what's happening externally by asking:
➤ Point 1: What am I hearing them say?
➤ Point 2: What am I seeing them do?
➤ Point 3: What am I sensing from their emotions and energy?

Second, notice what's happening inside you, by asking:
➤ Point 4: What am I hearing the still, small voice say?
➤ Point 5: What am I seeing in my mind's eye?
➤ Point 6: What am I sensing in my body/emotions?

When you are finished, end with a final request for information: "What do I need to do or say, in 'love' for the Highest Good of All?"

People often ask me how I know the difference between the voice of intuition or Spirit and the voice of rationalization. There is a distinct difference in the tone. The voice of intuition is a still, soft voice. Rationalization has a much harsher tone. That's why some people refer to it as "the chatter box." The voice of rationalization says, "Don't be foolish," "Don't take a chance and be wrong," "You could fail if you do that," or "They'll fire you from your job if you do." It's the voice of fear, loss, and shame.

Often times, intuition will guide us to say or do something that's contrary to what the ego-personality thinks it needs. The two greatest ego needs are to look good and to be right. For example, we may know we need to say a truth that will offend someone and cause him or her to judge us for speaking up. But if what we're saying comes from the heart and soul and is intended in "love," we need not worry. The intention is for the Highest Good of All. This approach doesn't promise immediate comfort or gratification, only that we'll all get exactly what we need.

Truth and love are the most important qualities to embody if we wish to manifest lives of peace. We must be truthful with ourselves as well as others. We must act on loving intentions. When we're living in the "L," we're automatically living in truth and love. In the "L," we're connected to self, intuitive wisdom, and God.

Being connected within gives us courage. Even when others react poorly to our truth, the stronger the connection to intuition, the more able we're to stand firm in word and deed. Through inner connection we have access to a secure sense of knowing and confidence that is unshakable.

When my brother and I went to my mother's for a second time to request information about my birth father, I was in a different emotional place. Because I was so thoroughly connected and living in the "L," she could sense that I was coming from compassion and non-judgment. This may have helped her feel safe to open up and tell the truth. At the first visit, I'd been consumed by my own feelings of fear, loss, and shame that I couldn't keep my heart open to her. I believe my mother could sense the shift in me, and that's part of the reason why she opened up. However, know that this is not always the outcome, no matter how loving you may be. It all depends on where the other person is in their journey, at the time.

When we trust intuition, we have greater mindfulness regarding the world around us. We feel less afraid. We have more courage, and the confidence to handle difficult people and situations. We notice cues at the "tip of the iceberg" that tell us we need to receive intuitive guidance. We then begin to get curious and ask for direction. A byproduct of greater awareness in the early stages is having time to slow down, ask, and wait until the answers come to us.

Tips for the Fourth Secret: How Might I Embrace a Love in Something Bigger that Myself?

Forgiveness was another lesson I learned in my journey to find the truth about my birthfather. I realized that when we forgive we experience freedom from the past. A pathway to a new beginning of thought, feeling, and behavior can then be established.

When forgiving, we need to remember everyone we

need to forgive: self, God, children, friends, co-workers, bosses, parents, and maybe even society or entire groups. When we forgive, we experience peace. Forgiveness means choosing to live in the energy of love, the "L". Forgiveness connects us more to self, intuitive wisdom, and Spirit than to the situation or a person whom we perceive caused us pain.

When we do not forgive, we stay attached to the victim/persecutor roles in our mind. This uses up the vital energy that otherwise could go towards manifesting our heart and soul's desire. We're consumed with thoughts like, "What did I do wrong?" "Why did God allow my dad to die?" "He did me wrong by keeping the secret!" When we stay attached to the victim/persecutor role by choosing to frame situations in this way, we feel drained instead of peaceful.

How can we know that we have unresolved anger that needs attention? We know we have not forgiven if we're holding onto thoughts such as, "They wronged me," "They did this to me," "I can't forgive someone who is so . . . ," " "I can't forgive because they won't work it out with me," " I am so bad," "They are so bad," and so on. If we hold these thoughts secretly in our minds, we need not judge ourselves for that. We simply need to plunge deeply into the emotion and then to ask for truth and the wisdom to show us what we need to learn.

Forgiveness isn't the same thing as forgetting, or sweeping, an issue under the carpet. Just because a situation is final, like a divorce, death, or leaving a job, doesn't mean we've forgiven. Thoughts let us know if we've forgiven. If we're holding onto thoughts that we or someone else is bad or wrong, we have not forgiven. If we are holding thoughts of punishment, retaliation, or pain for another, we have not forgiven.

I'll never forget the time that I had a radio talk show on WISN in Milwaukee. I was doing a program on "conflict resolution in the workplace." My guest was a

counselor and it was a live show for listeners to call-in
with their questions. One man called, and soon I
discovered, his call was not about conflict resolution in
the workplace at all. He began to complain that his wife
wasn't having sex with him frequently enough.

I was in total disbelief. How he got past my producer,
I'll never know! I couldn't help but wonder if someone was
playing a joke on me. I felt confused and scared. My first
inclination was to look at my guest and give him a nonverbal cue meaning, "This is your call." But he looked
back at me, eyes wide open, and shook his head no.

Knowing my guest was not willing to handle the call,
my only choice was to practice the One-Minute
Meditation. I took a deep breath and began the Six-Point
Check. What am I hearing the caller say? What am I
imagining him doing? What am I sensing from his
emotional energy? Because our interaction took place on
the radio, I had to rely on my mind's eye to give me a
picture of his body language. I had to trust my body to
be able to feel his emotional energy over the telephone
and airwaves. I took a deep breath. What came to me
were the words "shame" and "unforgiveness."

I continued to be curious. "Sir, I still am a bit
confused. Today's show is on conflict resolution. What
is your real question?" I asked in a loving voice. He
paused for a moment and then told me that he was in a
marriage where his wife was gone all the time. She often
left her teenage boy with him while she went out on the
town. I could hear the boy in the background acting out,
as he continued to share more of his story. He told me
that years earlier, before he was married to his current
wife, he was soon to become a doctor. One day, on the
way to his internship position, he got in a car accident
that left him paralyzed from the waist down. At that
time, he was engaged to another woman whom he loved
deeply. She left him.

I continued to breathe deeply as I listened to his

story. I stayed connected within and asked, *"What do I need to know?"* I heard a still, small voice tell me, "This is about forgiveness."

Feeling once again in the unknown and inadequate to handle this situation, I breathed even more deeply so as to connect more fully with self, my intuitive wisdom, and with God. I asked, "What do I need to do or say?" I heard, "Ask him if he forgave the person who hit him in the car."

"Did you forgive the person who hit you in the car?" I asked.

He responded, "I never had a chance to talk to him."

Still feeling inadequate, I went within and asked, *"Now what do I do or say?"*

This is what I heard that I needed to say: "I didn't ask if you talked to him, I asked if you forgave him." So, I said what I had been instructed to say in a low, slow, soft voice, following my intuition's lead.

He said exactly what I feared he would say. "I don't know how to do that."

There I was, live and on the air, in the unknown, way beyond my personal capabilities. My ego raced for a moment to its concerns: *Oh no . . . what will I say? Will I look stupid? What if I don't explain this right?* I knew my ego was trying to take over. I could feel the anxiety building in my body. Instead of giving in to it, I took a deep breath, and asked Higher Self to shed truth, love, and light on the situation.

I asked, *"How do I answer his question?"*

Then, I felt a warm, loving Spirit come over me. It told me what to say. *"Speak from your heart. Just share. Share with him when you felt betrayed in your life, and how it felt when you lost your dream. Share with him the process you had to go through to forgive yourself and those involved."*

Again, my ego did everything it could to stop me. The chatter box voice in my head went off, *"Don't make yourself look like a fool!"*

But I took another breath, deep into my body, noticed the voice, blessed it for wanting to protect my image, and told it, *"Thank you. Your job is now done. I AM choosing to connect with God and the Holy Spirit within me instead."*

So, with a DEEP breath . . . I began to share. I told him the story in this book of being deceived about my biological father and how going through the process of discovery was difficult for my husband and me. As a result of not being as emotionally or physically available to my husband as he had needed, our marriage fell apart. I also shared with the caller how this began a process of forgiveness for me. I forgave myself for not being able to extend myself during that time; my husband for not being able to sustain our marriage longer; God for allowing the pain; and my mother, birth father, and father for keeping the secret.

As he listened intently, I shared with him how I wrestled with God for some time, vacillating between anger, sadness, remorse, and shame. Eventually, it came to a point where I had to ask God to release me from pain and help me forgive. Eventually I had to ask to receive God's truth, love, and forgiveness, because it was beyond anything I could do on my own.

Choked up, he thanked me and said that was exactly what he needed. I understood. It was exactly what I needed too.

As it turned out, I felt so alive with the love of God within when I told him my story that I ended up writing this very book on my experience.

Who benefits the most through forgiveness? We do. When we forgive, we get better rather than becoming bitter. It enables us to see the blessings in our life, even if circumstances aren't as we hoped. Forgiveness takes us on a road trip back to living a life with our hearts wide open. By forgiving, we feel released, as we continue our journey with enough vital energy to manifest our heart and soul's purpose.

This was definitely true in my case. God allowed the secret and pain in my life to heal my lost relationship with myself, my connection to my intuition, and eventually learning to have a love in something bigger than myself. Working through my pain, using the process of forgiveness, brought me to my purpose.

The following forgiveness process was inspired by the book *Getting Bitter or Getting Better* by David W. Schell. Some of my steps are different, as I have added intuition and God into the formula. From my own experience, it's often difficult to forgive without establishing a connection within.

To begin the forgiveness process:

Select a current situation or person. What or who is it (yourself, another person, God, other)? Now, focus on this person or situation while you walk through the forgiveness steps. Ask your intuition and God to give you clarity and the power to forgive.

Step #1: Recognize the person or people you need to forgive in a situation. Include yourself and God if that feels true. Ask: Whom do I need to forgive?

Step #2: Recognize your state of mind and feelings. Ask: What am I honestly thinking and feeling?

Step #3: Tell God how you honestly feel about the situation. Don't hold back, even if some of your anger is directed toward God. Tell Him with all your heart and soul, "God, I am so (name your feeling) about (Name the situation or person)."

Let all your feelings out. Cry if you need to or punch a pillow if it helps. Writing out your feelings can also be helpful. There may be more than one person you need to forgive. Name them all. Go through this exercise with every person included in your situation.

Step #4: Recognize the effect your feeling has had on your life: Say, "By not forgiving, I am experiencing _____ in my life." (For example: bitterness, anger, the inability to move on, or an addiction.)

Step #5: Now, clear the deck, so that you can realize the truth. Request from your intuitive wisdom and God, "Show me a higher perspective and truth."

In your mind's eye, give up the victim or the persecutor role. Ask: "Show me how this was for the Highest Good of All." Or say, "Show me the lesson or the blessing in this situation."

Step #6: Make a commitment to being open, by saying, "I can and will be open to receive a new perspective on the situation."

Step #7: Pray for the power to forgive and release any negative feelings you are still holding. Sometimes it's difficult to let go because we believe these feelings have served to protect us. But that's an illusion. You begin to forgive by admitting your powerlessness. Ask God, "Help me to forgive and let go of any negative thoughts and feelings that I am holding that are not for the Highest good of All."

Step #8: Choose a new thought pattern. Say to yourself: "I AM seeing things from a Higher Perspective now. I AM able to see how this served my Highest Good and the Highest Good of All." Continue by saying, "My hurt and pain are over . . . I trust myself to choose what is most loving for myself and for the Highest Good of All."

Step #9: Choose a new way of being . . . choose to live in the "L," connected to your heart and to the love of God. Say, "I now feel re-connected with myself and God. I AM able to see how love was always there, even if it didn't appear that way on the surface."

Step #10: Take action. Ask God and your intuition how you need to move forward with this person or situation. Remember, just because you've forgiven doesn't mean you have forgotten. You can now make new choices in your situation because of the new truth you have received. To do this, Ask God and your intuition,

"What do I need to do or say, for the Highest Good of All, in my situation now that I have forgiven?"

This process may take time. Walk through the steps at a pace that works for you. Honor yourself exactly where you are in the process. Don't rush or judge yourself. Part of your healing is to receive God's unconditional love for being exactly as you are.

When you go through the Forgiveness Process, notice how it frees up your energy! Now, you can be more courageous, clear, and peaceful as you continue your life. Often you will even find purpose when you release the pain!

We're able to be grateful for the lessons of love in our situation when we focus on the question: "What did I need to learn from this experience to help me grow?" Although the situation may not have turned out as we originally hoped, we're able to see the unexpected gift when we ask to see the blessing and the lesson.

Transforming from fear to love and gratitude helps us courageously live our possibilities. Oftentimes, it is circumstances on the surface that look like failure or difficulty, which are actually our biggest heart and soul successes.

Instead of asking, "Why did this happen to me?" Ask, "What did I need to learn?" This question was helpful as my third husband and I began to reconcile. I thought that being able to forgive him for using pornography, let alone being with another woman, would be impossible. But when I learned about real forgiveness and the freedom it had to offer, I could see the situation from a different perspective. I was able to face my fear, and overcome it!

I'm not saying I was able to do this overnight. It took many conversations with Tom, a lot of praying, and some requirements for trust building as well. But, when I asked, "What did I need to learn?" I was able to transmute my own pain and realize: We are all sinners, and no sin is greater than any other.

Why do we sometimes miss the opportunity to be grateful for the lessons of love? We are operating from our ego-personality instead of Spirit. We are focused on getting what we want, versus being open to what our heart and soul really need. In my case, my biggest fears were deception and betrayal. Until I could let go of fear, I kept manifesting it in my life, as it was my "not" goal. All my efforts were going to "not" having that happen rather than towards creating love in my relationship. We have to sometimes face our biggest fear to overcome it. Moving from self-protection to an open heart of love, made a huge difference.

Our ego-personality, unlike Spirit, is concerned with things like comfort, feeling good, looking good, being right, and making things happen to suit our desires. The two unconscious concerns we are operating based on when we are on ego's path are "What's in it for me?" and "Make me feel important!" Many people have referred to ego by the acronym Edging God Out. I couldn't agree more.

When we lead lives connected with ourself, intuition, and God we have a different focus. Our concern is to do what is for the Highest Good of All, regardless of the price we need to pay or the sacrifice we have to make. That's a tall order in some cases, especially if we're attached to comfort and security. Enjoying and desiring things like money, a home, a nice job, a loving relationship, good health, and good looks are all fine goals. These things can certainly bring us pleasure, but when we hope that these things will fulfill us instead of looking to God to fulfill us, we have entered the battle within.

When we're focused on living in the "L" (the energy of love) in the littlest things, we continually ask the question, "What do I need to do or say, for the Highest

Good of All in this moment. I AM Yours!"

When we feel inner conflict and confusion, or don't even want to ask that question, it's because we're facing a battle between Spirit and our ego. When I think of this conflict, I picture a fork in the road in our moment-to-moment lives. With each decision we make, we get to choose our ego's desires or Spirit's needs.

Because God gives us free will, He allows us to choose ego's needs if that is what we think will make us happy. He does this because He knows that even if we chase illusions of happiness and fulfillment, once we "arrive" at our destination, we'll find ourselves empty still and wonder, "What else is there?" It's nearly impossible to feel deep gratitude and joy when we're chasing illusions. It's not to say we won't have times of happiness, they just don't last long or go very deep into our heart and soul when they arise from ego.

Once we realize we've been spending energy chasing ego desires, we must forgive ourselves for deceiving and betraying ourselves in situations that weren't for our highest good.

Don't beat yourself up when you get to this point down the road of human desires. Just notice it, forgive yourself, and get back on the right road.

Whenever I think of how to shift from ego to Spirit, I picture driving my car. Sometimes I can shift too quickly from third gear to fourth gear if I'm not paying attention. My car let's me know if it doesn't like that shift by making a squealing sound. That's kind of how it works for us when we get on the wrong path. Something inside us starts to squeal.

Are headaches, stomachaches, tension, anxiety, anger, discouragement, or depression trying to get your attention? Notice what your "inner engine" is telling you. Ask, "What do I need to learn to get back on the path of Spirit?"

One of the common ways that we get off the path of

Spirit is to hurry and make our lives busy most of the time. In fact, think about it. Nowadays, when you ask people how they are, they don't even say, "fine" anymore. Instead, they reply, "Oh, I'm so busy!" That's the ego screaming, "Look at me! Aren't I important . . . I'm so busy!"

Don't get me wrong. I've been guilty of that response and behavior plenty of times. The key is to notice when we're choosing busyness over trusting and allowing for God's love to work in our lives. When we trust and allow, we're once again connected and can live a life of peace and possibilities.

In my case, my busyness was a byproduct of my deep lack of trust in something bigger than myself. As the Bible says, "Be still and know that I AM God." When we surrender to the Great "I AM," and give up our own belief that "I am going to do or say this or that," then we truly begin to find our courage, clarity, and peace during our moment-to-moment circumstances.

When we choose to become conscious of whether our choices are based on fear or love, we become more in-tune with the path of Spirit. The universal lesson is to be self-aware as we make decisions even about the littlest matters.

Are your decisions based on truth and love or on fear and judgment?

I often reflect back to Leo Buscaglia's seminar on "Love," which I attended when I was 18 years old, and hearing a still, small voice tell me, "Someday, you too will have your own message on love." That message is about learning to embrace the love of God within in the littlest things.

How can you get connected with "love"? Begin to notice your humanness and typical reactive patterns, ask for help, and surrender. God is there. As you become more mindful, know that you're stretching your comfort zone. This process is like going to the gym to condition muscles you haven't worked out for a while. At first, it will feel uncomfortable. You may have an area in your life like me, where practicing this is more difficult. Although I am able to do this more easily at work, in my romantic relationships, it has been more of a challenge. Remember: No pain, no gain. Practice makes perfect!

As you begin to trust and allow more, and to claim the love of God within, you will find your ego reminding you "to look good and be right" and to focus on "What's in it for me?" or "Make me feel important!" Just notice these thoughts and reclaim "I AM love."

Another way to access the courage to live a life of love is to ask: "How can I be a vessel of love in this situation for the Highest Good of All?" When we focus our minds on that question, and open our hearts in gratitude for the love we already have within, we find the answer. Remember: Thoughts create feelings, feelings create actions, and actions create results. If you want to live a life of love, change your thoughts and focus your intention on love.

Many of us end up not being vessels of love at work or at home when faced with difficult situations or difficult people. It is always easier to love the lovable, isn't it? When others are in their reactive patterns, it is tempting to go into our victim/persecutor roles. We feel justified and tell ourselves, "I am no one's doormat!" When we feel self-righteous in our anger, we miss the opportunity to be vessels of love.

Reactive patterns are habitual. Be forgiving of yourself as you learn. This will be your bridge of compassion for others as they're learning their lessons.

At this point in our journey, we realize that what we do isn't as important as how we go about doing it. We become more aware of how we respond in a situation and define ourselves from an internal way of being versus our external conditions.

When we live in the "I AM" presence our identity is

clear: We are love.

There is great freedom, peace, and fulfillment when we shift our focus from "Who am I?" to the Great "I AM." Living a passionate and fulfilling life no longer has anything to do with what we acquire or what the outcomes are in our life. It also doesn't have anything to do with what others think. Instead, we are defined by our connection within and our responses to life. As we share the love and abundance within us, we open our hearts to love and give it away with ease.

Now it's time to bring it back to you . . . Take the following test and see how you do.

How Well Do You Practice the Four Secrets to "I AM"?
(Circle the letter that best describes you)

1. How do you show sympathy for another person?
    a.   By saying, "I see what you mean."
    b.   By telling them, "I understand."
    c.   By relating to the experience and sharing it with them.

2. If someone asked you about your favorite restaurant, you would first:
    a.   Picture what it looked like.
    b.   Explain to them what was on the menu.
    c.   Recall how you felt at the restaurant, remember your experience, and the taste of the food.

3. If you were in a meeting with co-workers who didn't agree on an issue, you would:
    a.   Get an idea, but never verbalize it, because you told yourself, "It would never work."
    b.   Try to convince others why your idea would work.
    c.   Try to get in touch with what idea felt right to you, and then confidently express the idea.

4. If you thought a loved one was lying to you, you would:

    a. Recognize your hunches, and quickly ask them about your doubts.

    b. Doubt your hunches until you had enough proof.

    c. Trust your hunches and peacefully wait for inner guidance.

5. If you had a big decision to make at work, you would:

    a. Picture each of the possibilities, including asking others for their opinions.

    b. Gather as much information as possible, including asking others for their opinions.

    c. Consider the options, while focusing on how you felt emotionally and physically about each one of them.

6. Regarding your eating habits, do you?

    a. Wing it, but in general follow the food pyramid.

    b. Plan your meals in advance and adhere to them strictly.

    c. Stop and listen to what your body says it needs.

7. What do you do when you see your body naked in the mirror?

    a. Run.

    b. Find something negative about it and tell yourself you need to change.

    c. Feel appreciative and accepting regardless of your body image.

8. When you have a headache, do you?

    a. Ignore it and hope it goes away.

    b. Take aspirin and "keep on plugging."

    c. Stop, relax, and get in touch with what the possible cause might be.

9. If a co-worker embarrasses you in a meeting, do you?
   a. Feel like you could cry, but tell yourself not to be silly, "You're over-reacting."
   b. Call a friend later and repeat the conversation word-for-word, until you're done venting.
   c. Feel the embarrassment and take time after the meeting to get in touch with what it meant to you.

10. If time passed and you were still torn on a big decision, you would:
    a. Analyze the decision to find the best choice.
    b. Ask others to give their input for the greatest "buy-in."
    c. Take time to reflect, have a positive expectancy, and then trust the answer will be there.

Now, score your quiz.

Now, let's see how you did! Add up your points.
Each a = 1 point, each b = 3 points, and each c = 5 points.

41-50 Points: You Live the Four Secrets! You connect with yourself, your intuition, and your Higher Power well! You understand what it means to surrender to something bigger than yourself, for the Highest Good of all! Congratulations! You are living the Four Secrets most often!

35-40 Points: You Practice the Four Secrets Often!

More often than not, you connect with yourself, your intuition, and your Higher Power. From time to time you may push away your gut feelings and yourself, but that is only when things get chaotic for you. It usually is when you are attached to a certain outcome. The good news is that you learn quickly from your tendencies. Keep re-opening your heart, staying aware, and surrendering.

30-34: You Are Aware at Some Level That the Four Secrets Exist!

You are like most people and connect with yourself, intuitive wisdom, and your Higher Power when you are not busy or anxious. There are times you know, but don't trust yourself or God. You tend to push the still, small voice away, and try to take control of your life instead. To improve, slow down and breathe more deeply. Meditate on God's power and love in your life. Make a conscious decision to embrace the intuitive wisdom that is there for you to show you the cues at the "tip of the Iceberg." Remember to request, "Show me the love and lessons here."

20-29: You Have a Desire to Build Your Connection with the Four Secrets!

It is not that you aren't at all connected to your emotions, your intuition, or God. It is just that you need to trust and let go more. It's like going to the gym to work out. If you don't naturally have a strong abdomen, you have to do a few extra sit-ups to build those muscles. It's the same with learning to keep your heart open to life and a power greater than you. Focus intention on it and it will build. Keep a journal to see your progress! Note chaotic situations that are trying to get your attention. Surrender control by asking, "What is real and true here?" and "What do I need to do or say for the Highest Good of all?"

About the Author

Susan K. Wehrley is the president of Susan K. Wehrley & Associates, an organization headquartered in Brookfield, Wisconsin. Her Mission is to "Empower Individuals and Company Leaders to become more Effective in their Business and Professional Life."

Established in 1988, her company specializes in training and development for leaders, employees, and individuals desiring to improve skills in sales, customer service, teamwork, leadership, and personal empowerment. Susan incorporates techniques that enhance intuitive wisdom in all of her programs. It is her belief that in order to be effective and manifest our goals, we must use our intuition and gut instincts. By connecting with intuitive wisdom, we can notice "tip of the iceberg" cues and make choices that are in synch with our destiny. She also believes that we must be connected with the "I AM" presence in order to live on purpose.

For more information on Susan K. Wehrley's books, programs, and services, please visit her website: www.thesecrettoIAM.com, or telephone: (262) 785-8188. You may also e-mail her at info@thesecrettoIAM.com. For information on her training programs, see her website: www.solutionsbysusan.com.

Personal Notes

Personal Notes

Personal Notes

Personal Notes

Personal Notes

Personal Notes

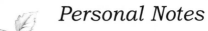

Personal Notes

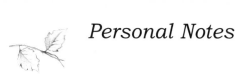

Personal Notes

Books and Products to Order

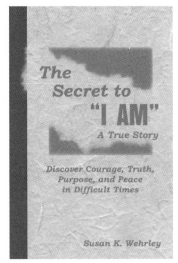

Travel with the author as she discovers her biological identity and the Four Secrets that led her to a life of inner fulfillment.

The Secret to "I AM"
A True Story
ISBN: 0-9729505-0-8
Adhesive Bound, Hard Cover Book
Retail Price: $19.95

Discover your unique story and life's purpose with this easy to follow Journal to self-discovery.

The Secret to "I AM"
Journal
ISBN: 0-9729505-1-6
Fully Concealed twin loop, Hard Cover Book
Retail Price: $16.95

Also Available in Limited Keepsake Edition:
ISBN 0-9729505-2-4   Retail Price: $45.95
Both books shown above are included in the keepsake edition. Made with all natural handmade paper and a special message to the receiver of the set. Comes in a beautiful matching all natural box to make this a real keepsake!

The Secret to "I AM"
Wisdom Tips and Workbook
ISBN 0-9729505-3-2   Retail Price: $24.95

Audio Programs
The Secret to "I AM"
Wisdom Tips CD
ISBN: 0-9729505-4-0 Retail Price: $12.95

Videotapes
The Secret to "I AM"
Sensory Seminar
ISBN: 0-9729505-5-9 Retail Price: $35.95

Published by

Thomas
& Kay

To Order: Phone 262-785-8188
website: www.thesecrettoIAM.com
e-mail: info@thesecrettoIAM.com